Fo
Acapulco

Anya Schiffrin

Fodor's Travel Publications, Inc.
New York and London

ISBN 0–679–01625–2

Fodor's Acapulco

Editor: Kathleen McHugh
Researchers: Erica Meltzer, Frank Shiell
Art Director: Fabrizio La Rocca
Cartographer: David Lindroth
Illustrator: Karl Tanner
Cover Photograph: Morton Beebe

Design: Vignelli Associates

About the Author

Anya Schiffrin is a well-traveled freelance writer who left for London, Spain, and Pakistan soon after completing this assignment. She has been published in the *Village Voice*, and British publications such as *City Limits*, *Time Out*, *New Society*, and *Hot Air*, Virgin Atlantic Airline's inflight magazine.

Special Sales

Contents

Foreword

"Nirvana by the Sea," "Miami on the Pacific," and "Queen of the Mexican Resorts" are among the phrases that have, at one time or another, been used to describe Acapulco, the archetypal beachgoer's destination. Legendary haven for the jet-set, politicians, and literary greats, Acapulco today attracts those of more modest means seeking almost-guaranteed sunshine; bargains in silver, leather, and Mexican handicrafts; and the frenzied nightlife of lore.

The falling peso and Acapulco's proximity to the United States make Acapulco even more attractive as a vacation option to those "north of the border," especially in winter. This guide presents the widest range of sights, activities, restaurants, and accommodations, and within that range, selections that are worthwhile and of the best value. The descriptions provided are just enough for you to make your own informed choices from among our selections.

This is an exciting time for Fodor's, as it begins a three-year program to rewrite, reformat, and redesign all 140 of its guides. Here are just a few of the exciting new features:

★ Brand-new computer-generated maps locating all the top attractions, hotels, restaurants, and shops

★ A unique system of numbers and legends to help readers move effortlessly between text and maps

★ A new star rating system for hotels and restaurants

★ Restaurant reviews by major food critics around the world

★ Stamped, self-addressed postcards, bound into every guide, give readers an opportunity to help evaluate hotels and restaurants

★ Complete page redesign for instant retrieval of information

★ FODOR'S CHOICE—Our favorite museums, beaches, cafes, romantic hideaways, festivals, and more

★ HIGHLIGHTS '89—An insider's look at the most important developments in tourism during the past year

★ TIME OUT—The best and most convenient lunch stops along the shopping and exploring routes

★ Exclusive background essays create a powerful portrait of each destination

★ A mini-journal for travelers to keep track of their own itineraries and addresses

While every care has been taken to assure the accuracy of the information in this guide, the passage of time will always bring change, and consequently, the publisher cannot accept responsibility for errors that may occur.

All prices and opening times quoted here are based on information available to us at press time. Hours and admission fees may change, however, and the prudent traveler will avoid inconvenience by calling ahead.

Fodor's wants to hear about your travel experiences, both pleasant and unpleasant. When a hotel or restaurant fails to live up to its billing, let us know and we will investigate the complaint and revise our entries where the facts warrant it.

Send your letters to the editors of Fodor's Travel Publications, 201 E. 50th Street, New York, NY 10022, or 30-32 Bedford Square, London WC1B 3SG, England.

Highlights '89 and Fodor's Choice

Highlights '89

Though situated in the heart of mañana land, much is happening in Acapulco, both positive and negative. First the bad news. On April 12, 1988, the government-owned airline, **Aeroméxico,** suspended service as a result of a strike of ground personnel at its Mexico City hub. The national carrier filed for bankruptcy a few days later, wreaking havoc with travelers holding tickets on Aeroméxico flights and forcing others to find alternate flights. At press time, the FAA was allowing the other carriers to Mexico, such as Mexicana, American, Continental and Northwest, to increase their capacity, but not add extra routes. The apportionment of routes covered by Aeroméxico must be approved by both the U.S. and Mexican governments.

Also at press time, there are rumblings that the peso, the Mexican unit of currency, which is now 2,290 to the U.S. dollar will be **devalued.** Coins minted recently have no lettering on them, adding fuel to the rumors that when devalued, the peso will be renamed the **azteca.**

Though many come to Acapulco to frolic in the Bay of Acapulco, don't be tempted by the allure of the blue water. The **pollution problem,** a result of poor or little sewage treatment, is worse than ever. Signs are now posted on some of the more exclusive beaches warning bathers about the hazards of the water, and incidents of dysentery have been reported. Take a cue from the Mexican cognoscenti and take to the water of your hotel pool.

On the hotel front, **Playa Secreto,** on Punta Guitarrón near Las Brisas, continues to have construction problems, though open since December 1986. The isolated Sheraton property will eventually have its own tram to take guests between the 17 buildings, two pools, a disco, and two tennis courts. But long waits for transport and a shortage of some catering items, compounded by the din of on-going construction, suggest that the opening of this Sheraton was premature.

Now for some good news: The **revitalization of Traditional Acapulco,** bandied about for a couple of years, is finally underway. Traditional Acapulco is synonymous with downtown, an area that *was* Acapulco some 50 years ago. The town's first hotels were built here in the hills to take advantage of the cooling sea breezes. But as newer properties sprung up along the Costera Miguel Alemán, Traditional Acapulco grew seedy. The 300-room Hotel Caleta, on Caleta Beach, has been renovated and the Hotel Club de Pesca, slated for reconstruction back in 1985, will be rebuilt. Other properties scheduled for upgrading include El Mirador, Del Monte, and Los Flamingos.

One of the features of the rebirth of Traditional Acapulco should alleviate the other beach problem—hordes of **strolling vendors** who sometimes hound those who'd rather sunbathe in peace. The vendors are being paid to relocate to public markets where they will have stalls to conduct their business.

In the same vein, the modern **charro** ring where *charreadas* (Mexican-style rodeos) are held is being promoted. Located near the airport, the two-year-old ring is the site of steer-wrestling and bronco-busting matches. The major participants are men—physicians, architects, and attorneys in real life who play cowboy—though women sometimes participate.

The **Mexican National Tourism Office in Acapulco** (SECTUR), is no longer across from the Centro Internacional de Convivencia Infantil (CiCi). The new location is Costera 187 (tel. 748/5–13–04). Also the Centro Acapulco, Acapulco's convention center, has been renamed the Centro Internacional.

The glass-lined **Marbella Mall** is Acapulco's newest shopping showcase. Near the Diana Glorieta, it opened in April 1988 and is host to a variety of upscale shops and eateries. **El Fuerte del Virrey,** behind Carlos 'n Charlie's restaurant at Roca Sola 17, stole the limelight the second it opened—it was featured in Mexico's major lifestyle magazine. Inside this unusual antique-filled building designed as an 18th-century fort, is a military museum and four restaurants: The rooftop *Povorin* has ribs and salads; *Taberna* specializes in champagne and international seafood delights such as *gravlax*, a Swedish dish of cured salmon and lobster tails; *La Ropa* has live music and Mexican cuisine; and *El Real* (*see* Dining) has already joined the ranks of Acapulco's top restaurants.

Fodor's Choice

No two people will agree on what makes a perfect vacation, but it's fun—and it can be helpful—to know what others think. Here, then, is a very personal list of Fodor's Choices. We hope you'll have a chance to experience some of them yourself while visiting Acapulco. We have tried to offer something for everyone and from every price category. For detailed information about each entry, refer to the appropriate chapters within this guidebook.

Special Moments

Dancing under the stars at Discobeach

Fireworks at Fantasy Disco

Drinking a popper

Seeing Coyuca Lagoon for the first time

The view of the bay from Miramar

Taste Treats

Cheeseburgers at Mimi's Chili Saloon

Yogurt fruit shakes at 100% Natural

Tacos from a street vendor

Grilled *huachinango* (red snapper) at beach restaurants

Chilled summery soups at Madeiras

Cold beer and chips at Zorrito's

After Hours

A night cruise on the *Aca Tiki*

Cats Disco, especially on $10 all-you-can-drink nights

Mexican fiesta and mariachis at the Calinda Hotel

Sunset at Pie de la Cuesta

Champagne boat ride to see the cliff divers

Off the Beaten Track

Breakfast at the Zócalo

Boat rides on the lagoon at Barra Vieja

Mass at Nuestra Señora de la Soledad

Exploring the market downtown

Best Restaurants

El Real (*Expensive*)

Madeiras (*Moderate*)

Pinzona 65 (*Moderate*)

Tlaquepaque (*Inexpensive*)

Zorrito's (*Inexpensive*)

Best Hotels

Villa Vera (*Very Expensive*)

Acapulco Plaza (*Expensive*)

Pierre Marqués (*Expensive*)

Maralisa (*Moderate*)

Playa Hermosa (*Inexpensive*)

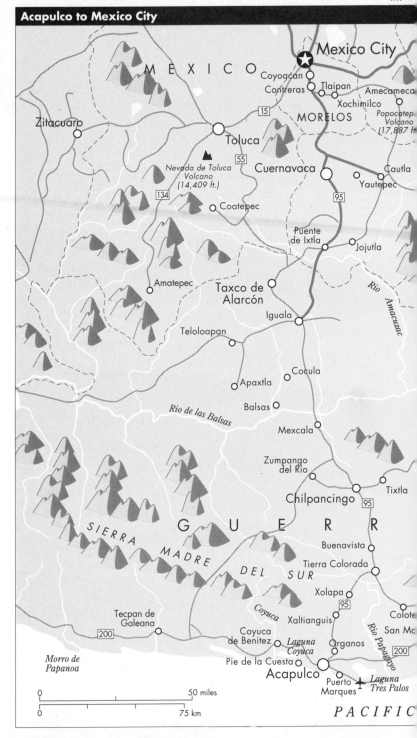

Acapulco to Mexico City

Mexico City

M E X I C O

Coyoacán
Contreras
Tlaipan
Amecameca
Xochimilco

MORELOS

Popocatep.
Volcano
(17,887 ft)

Zitacuaro

15

Toluca

55

Nevada de Toluca
Volcano
(14,409 ft.)

Cuernavaca

Cautla
Yautepec

134

Coatepec

95

Puente
de Ixtla

Jojutla

Rio Amacuzac

Amatepec

Taxco de
Alarcón

Iguala

Teloloapan

Apaxtla

Cocula

Balsas

Rio de las Balsas

Mexcala

Zumpango
del Rio

Chilpancingo

95

Tixtla

S I E R R A

G   U   E   R   R

M A D R E

Buenavista

D E L   S U R

Tierra Colorada

Xolapa

95

Colote

San Mc

Rio Papagayo

Coyuca

Tecpan de
Galeana

200

Xaltianguis

Coyuca
de Benitez
Laguna
Coyuca

Organos

200

Morro de
Papanoa

Pie de la Cuesta

Acapulco

Puerto
Marques

Laguna
Tres Palos

0   50 miles

0   75 km

P A C I F I C

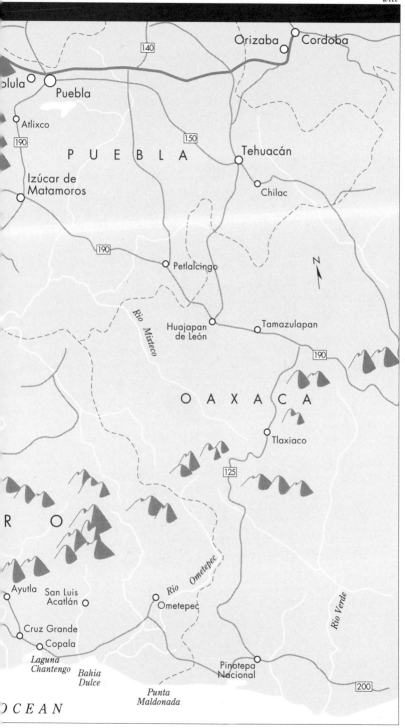

World Time Zones

Numbers below vertical bands relate each zone to Greenwich Mean Time (0 hrs.).
Local times frequently differ from these general indications,
as indicated by light-face numbers on map.

Auckland, **1**	Denver, **8**	New York City, **16**	Rio de Janeiro, **23**
Honolulu, **2**	Chicago, **9**	Washington, DC, **17**	Buenos Aires, **24**
Anchorage, **3**	Dallas, **10**	Miami, **18**	Reykjavik, **25**
Vancouver, **4**	New Orleans, **11**	Bogotá, **19**	Dublin, **26**
San Francisco, **5**	Mexico City, **12**	Lima, **20**	London (Greenwich), **27**
Los Angeles, **6**	Toronto, **13**	Santiago, **21**	Lisbon, **28**
Edmonton, **7**	Ottawa, **14**	Caracas, **22**	Algiers, **29**
	Montreal, **15**		Paris, **30**
			Zürich, **31**

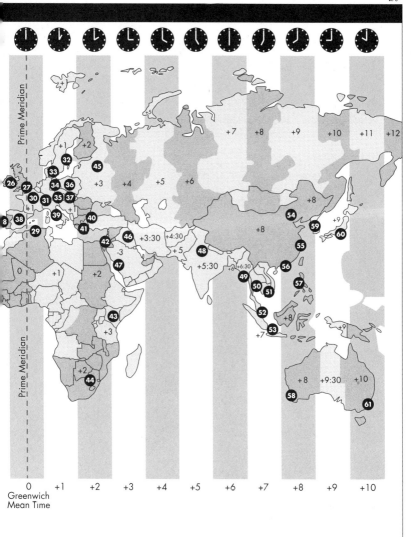

Stockholm, **32**
Copenhagen, **33**
Berlin, **34**
Vienna, **35**
Warsaw, **36**
Budapest, **37**
Madrid, **38**

Rome, **39**
Istanbul, **40**
Athens, **41**
Jerusalem, **42**
Nairobi, **43**
Johannesburg, **44**
Moscow, **45**
Baghdad, **46**

Mecca, **47**
Delhi, **48**
Rangoon, **49**
Bangkok, **50**
Saigon, **51**
Singapore, **52**
Djakarta, **53**
Beijing, **54**
Shanghai, **55**

Hong Kong, **56**
Manila, **57**
Perth, **58**
Seoul, **59**
Tokyo, **60**
Sydney, **61**

Introduction

For sun lovers, beach bums, and other hedonists, Acapulco is the ideal holiday resort. Don't expect high culture, historic monuments, or haute cuisine. Anyone who ventures to this Pacific resort 200 miles southwest of Mexico City does so to relax. Translate that as swimming, shopping, and nightlife.

Everything takes place against a staggeringly beautiful natural backdrop. Acapulco Bay is one of the world's best natural harbors, and it is the city's centerpiece. By day the water looks clean and temptingly deep blue; at night it flashes and sparkles with the city lights. Just eating *quesadillas* by the bay becomes a glamorous experience simply because the setting is so stunning.

Added to Acapulco's attraction is the exchange rate. Mexico is one of the few countries in the world where the dollar has not taken a beating in the past year. In fact, recent devaluations of the peso mean that some prices have actually come down. While the weak peso and a crippling inflation rate (at this writing it tops 160% a year) make life for the Mexicans a misery, the visitor will find that a little hard currency goes a long way. Acapulco is an ideal destination for the budget-minded. There are plenty of hotels where a double room is less than $50 and dozens of small eateries, usually family-run, where three courses and drinks rarely exceed $10.

The weather is Acapulco's major draw—warm waters, almost constant sunshine, and year-round temperatures in the 80s. It comes as no surprise, then, that most people plan their day around laying their towel on some part of Acapulco's many miles of beach. Both tame and wild water sports are available—everything from waterskiing to snorkeling, diving, and the thrill of parasailing. Less-strenuous possibilities are motorboat rides and fishing trips. Championship golf courses, tennis courts, and the food/crafts markets also occasionally lure some visitors away from the beach, but not out of the sun.

Apart from these options, most people rouse themselves from their hammock, deck chair, or towel only when it is feeding time. Eating is one of Acapulco's great pleasures. You will find that in most dishes the ingredients are very fresh. Seafood is caught locally, and restaurateurs go to the *mercado* (market) daily to select the produce, meats, and fish for that night's meals. Best of all are the no-frills, down-home Mexican restaurants. Prices are reasonable and the food in these family-run places is prepared with care—spiced soups filled with red snapper (and red snapper heads), baskets filled with hot corn tortillas instead of bread. Eating at one of these spots gives you a glimpse into the real Mexico: office workers breaking for lunch, groups of men socializing over a cup of coffee. Even at a little greasy spoon you can eat very well for $5. Those with strong stomachs will discover, too, that it is quite possible to eat a plate of 50¢ tacos from a street vendor without being rushed immediately to the hospital.

At night, Acapulco is transformed as the city rouses itself from the day's torpor and prepares for the long hours ahead.

Even though Acapulco's heyday is past, its nightlife is legendary. This is true despite the fact that the city's 10 major discos all look like they were designed in the early '70s by an architect who bought mirrors and strobe lights wholesale. Perpetually crowded, the discos are grouped in twos and threes, so most people go to several places in one night. Last year's disco hits and huge fruity cocktails are trademarks of the Acapulco disco experience.

Acapulco was originally an important port for the Spanish, who used it to trade with countries in the Far East. They built Fuerte de San Diego (Fort San Diego) to protect the city from pirates, and today the fort houses a historical museum with exhibits about Acapulco's past.

The name of Teddy Stauffer, an entrepreneurial Swiss, is practically synonymous with that of modern Acapulco. He hired the first cliff divers at La Quebrada in Old Acapulco, and founded the Boom Boom Room, the town's first dance hall, and Tequila A Go-Go, its first discotheque. The Hotel Mirador at La Quebrada and the area stretching from Caleta to Hornos beaches, near today's Old Acapulco, were the center of activity in the 1950s, when Acapulco was a town of 20,000 with an economy based largely on fishing.

Former President Miguel Alemán Valdes bought up miles of the coast just before the road and the airport were built. The Avenida Costera Miguel Alemán bears his name today. Since the late 1940s, Acapulco has expanded eastward so that it is today one of Mexico's largest cities, with a population of approximately 2 million. The next area slated for development is Punta Diamante (Diamond Point), between the Barra Vieja and Revolcadero Beach in the East Bay. It should be ready for visitors by the end of the century.

Acapulco is laid out very neatly. Almost everything takes place on the Avenida Costera Miguel Alemán, the wide boulevard that hugs the shoreline. From the airport going west you come first to the East Bay, which is home to the most expensive hotels, the Princess, Pierre Marqués, and Las Brisas, a Westin property. Fantasy—the most elegant of all the discos—is here, next to La Vista shopping center, as are the prestigious Madeiras and Miramar restaurants. Going down the scenic highway from the East Bay you come to the naval base and the Hyatt Regency. This marks the beginning of The Strip, which is the touristy area of town. All the luxury hotels, most of the restaurants popular with Americans and Canadians, and the luxury stores and discos are here, as are all the airline offices and car rental agencies. The area around the Condesa Hotel is at the thick of things. Once you get to the American Express office, things slow down until you reach the Diana Glorieta (traffic circle). The Acapulco Plaza and Ritz hotels and a cluster of five discos stretch between the Diana and Papagayo Park. The park signals the end of The Strip. From there you pass a few hotels and beach restaurants and Fuerte de San Diego. On the right is the Central Post Office and the Zócalo (the main plaza). This marks the heart of Old Acapulco. Woolworth's, small tailors, inexpensive seafood restaurants, several markets, and the doctors' offices are here. Cruise ships and fishing boats leave from the dock near the Zócalo. Five minutes northwest of the Zócalo is La Quebrada, where the cliff divers daily perform their daring leaps. A few minutes more down the Costera is Caleta Beach, where you catch the ferry to Roqueta Island.

A relaxed, holiday atmosphere pervades Acapulco; shorts and T-shirts comprise the dress code, and many visitors go home with a full address book. People strike up conversations on the beach, in bars, and with whomever is eating dinner at the next table. The Mexicans you meet are friendly and will always help out with directions on the street or in the post office. Many travelers return to Acapulco every year to catch up on friendships begun on a previous vacation. The only drawback to this laid-back air is that things aren't done on a fixed schedule. Everything from car rentals to purchases takes much longer than you might expect. But there is no point in getting annoyed—just sit back and relax while you wait.

1 Planning Your Trip

Before You Go

Government Tourist Offices

Contact the Mexican Government Tourism Office for brochures, lists of special events, and transportation schedules.

In the United States. 405 Park Ave., Suite 1002, New York, NY 10022, tel. 212/755–7261; 1616 L St. NW, Suite 430, Washington, DC 20036, tel. 202/659–8730; 70 E. Lake St., Suite 1413, Chicago, IL 60601, tel. 312/565–2786; 10100 Santa Monica Blvd., Suite 224, Los Angeles, CA 90067, tel. 213/203–9335; 2707 N. Loop West, Suite 450, Houston, TX 77008, tel. 713/880–5153.

In Canada. 1 Place Ville Marie, Suite 2409, Montreal, Quebec H3B 3M9, tel. 514/871–1052; 181 University Ave., Suite 1112, Toronto, Ontario M5H 3M7, tel. 416/364–2455.

In the United Kingdom. 7 Cork St., London W1X 7PB England, tel. 441/734–1058.

Tour Groups

Mexico remains one of the few real travel bargains available these days. The weak peso and the buying power of tour operators combine to create some very attractively priced packages. In Acapulco, independent packages are the typical way to go, because everything is pretty much in one place and getting to sights is relatively easy. Group tours are more common for interior and special-interest programs. Tours linking Mexico City and Acapulco may start out as a group program in Mexico City and then offer free time on the coast. Below is a sampling of tour operators with packages in the region. For additional resources, contact your travel agent and/or the Mexican Government Tourism Office.

Before booking a tour, find out: exactly what expenses are included (particularly tips, taxes, side trips, additional meals, and entertainment); government ratings of all hotels on the itinerary and the facilities they offer; cancellation policies for both you and for the tour operator; and, if you are traveling alone, the cost of a single supplement. Most tour operators request that bookings be made through a travel agent—there is no additional charge.

General-Interest Tours

American Express Vacations (Box 5014, Atlanta, GA 30302, tel. 800/241–1700 or in Georgia, 800/282–0800) is a veritable supermarket of tours.

Liberty Travel/Gogo Tours (50 A&S Drive, Paramus, NJ 07652, tel. 201/967–3000) moved more than 170,000 travelers through Mexico last year, with a wide selection of tours at prices from budget to bonanza.

Mexico Travel Advisors (1717 N. Highland Ave., Los Angeles, CA 90028, tel. 213/462–5345) has been leading tours to Mexico for 57 years.

Other popular operators include: **American Leisure** (9800 Center Pkwy., Suite 800, Houston, TX 77036, tel. 800/777–1980 or 713/988–6098 in Texas) and **Friendly Holidays** (118-21 Queens

Blvd., Forest Hills, NY 11375, tel. 800/221–9748). All offer Acapulco packages.

Package Deals for Independent Travelers

All of the tour operators listed above offer air/hotel packages. There are literally dozens of nearly identical packages to Mexico City, Acapulco, or a combination of the two. Your travel agent should be able to steer you to the ones using reliable airlines and respectable hotels.

When to Go

The weather in Acapulco is basically the same all year, with an average temperature of 80°F (or 27°C). The hottest months are June, July, and August; the coolest is January. During high season, December 15 to Easter, it rarely rains. The summer is more humid, August and October being the rainiest months. Whatever the time of year, you never need a jacket or a wrap, and the water is always warm. Low season (July to October) offers the advantage of lower prices and less people, though some restaurants and hotels close for vacation or to make repairs.

November is considered a "shoulder" month. Prices will be midway between those in effect in high and low seasons. But even in low season, tour operators fill up the biggest hotels. The peak time for crowds is December 25 to January 3, when you may have trouble booking a hotel room. *Semana Santa*, the week before Easter, is very popular with Mexicans; schools are in recess and families come to Acapulco for their children's vacation. Budget hotels get very noisy and many tourists party all night and sleep on the beaches. Remember, no matter when you want to visit, book ahead to avoid disappointment.

Climate The following are the average daily maximum and minimum temperatures for Acapulco.

Jan.	88F	31C	May	90F	32C	Sept.	90F	32C
	72	22		77	25		75	24
Feb.	88F	31C	June	91F	33C	Oct.	90F	32C
	72	22		77	25		75	24
Mar.	88F	31C	July	90F	32C	Nov.	90F	32C
	72	22		77	25		73	23
Apr.	90F	32C	Aug.	91F	33C	Dec.	88F	31C
	73	23		77	25		72	22

Current weather information on 235 cities around the world— 180 of them in the United States—is only a phone call away. To obtain the Weather Trak telephone number for your area, call 800/247–3282. The local number plays a taped message that tells you to dial the three-digit access code for the destination you're interested in. The code is either the area code (in the United States) or the first three letters of the foreign city. For a list of all access codes, send a stamped, self-addressed envelope to Cities, Box 7000, Dallas, TX 75209. For further information, phone 214/869–3035 or 800/247–3282.

Festivals and Seasonal Events

The following is a sampling of the top festivals held annually in Acapulco. For additional information, contact the **Mexican Government Tourism Office**, 405 Park Ave., Suite 1002, New York, NY 10022, tel. 212/755–7261 or 838–2949.

Jan. 1: New Year's Day is celebrated throughout Mexico. In the provinces, many agricultural and livestock fairs take place.

Jan. 6: Feast of Epiphany is the day the Three Kings bring gifts to children throughout Mexico.

Feb. 2: Candlemas Day, or the Blessing of Candles, is celebrated nationwide, with fiestas, fairs, and lantern-decorated streets.

Feb. 5: Constitution Day is a national holiday commemorating the National Charter, which officially ended the Revolution of 1910, giving birth to modern Mexico.

Late Feb. or early Mar.: Carnival is celebrated throughout the country with colorful parades and fiestas.

Mar. 21: Benito Juarez's Birthday is a national holiday.

Week before Easter: Holy Week (Semana Santa) means processions, services, and other events, culminating on Easter Sunday.

May 1: Labor Day is a national holiday with workers' parades.

May 3: Holy Cross Day is observed nationwide by construction workers, who place decorated crosses atop unfinished buildings.

May 5: Cinco de Mayo is the anniversary of the French defeat at Puebla in 1862.

May 15: Feast of San Isidro Labrador is celebrated nationwide with the blessing of new seeds and animals.

June 1: Navy Day is commemorated in all seaports in Mexico and is especially colorful in Acapulco.

June 24: Saint John the Baptist Day is a national holiday.

July 16: Feast of the Virgin del Carmen is a holiday celebrated across Mexico with fiestas, pilgrimages, and religious rites.

Late July: Feast of Santiago is a national holiday that features Mexican-style rodeos.

Aug. 15: Feast of the Assumption of the Blessed Virgin Mary is celebrated nationwide with religious processions.

Sept. 15–16: Independence Day is when all of Mexico reaffirms independence. The biggest celebrations are held in Mexico City.

Oct. 4: Feast of St. Francis of Assisi is commemorated nationwide with processions and parties.

Oct. 12: Columbus Day is observed throughout all Mexico.

Nov. 1: All Saints Day includes religious rites and processions throughout the country.

Nov. 2: All Souls Day is a time to honor the dead nationwide.

Nov. 20: Anniversary of the Mexican Revolution is observed as a national holiday.

Dec. 12: Feast Day of the Virgin of Guadalupe is when the patron saint of the nation is honored.

Dec. 16–25: Christmas season is highlighted with nightly processions and *piñatas*. Christmas Eve and Christmas Day are family holidays.

What to Pack

Pack light, because the bargains are hard to resist. If you're like most tourists to Mexico, your luggage will be considerably heavier on your trip home. The luggage restrictions on flights from the United States to Mexico are the same as for domestic United States flights. You are allowed either two pieces of check-in luggage and two pieces of carry-on, or three pieces of check-in, and one carry-on. Carry-on luggage cannot exceed 45 inches (length + width + height). If you carry on two, one cannot exceed 70 pounds and the other, 50 pounds. If you check in three, each can weigh up to 70 pounds. The first bag cannot exceed 65 inches (length + width + height), the second, 55 inches and the third, 45 inches.

Clothing Acapulco is very informal. Pack as you would for any beach resort that has extremely hot, humid weather. Leave suits, ties, and fancy clothes at home. Concentrate on light cotton clothes and a bathing suit. Shorts, T-shirts, and separates are what most people wear. At night, men turn up in slacks and shirts, and women dress up a bit more, usually in cotton dresses or skirts and blouses. But except for what's fashionable at the discos and the better restaurants, the Acapulco look is very casual; not even at the top places does anyone wear a tie or anything that could be termed "formal." Women should pack just a couple of simple accessories to jazz up their day wear, which will provide a quick conversion from casual to casual-but-elegant. With the exclusion of shoes and lingerie, you can buy anything you need in Acapulco, often dirt-cheap.

Miscellaneous Women should take along all their favorite **cosmetics,** including nail polish and shampoo; you can't be sure you'll find your brand or your shade. Forget **hair spray, mousse,** and **gel**; they get sticky in the heat and are magnets for mosquitoes. A **small calculator** helps to figure out prices on the spot. Many department stores sell currency converter calculators. If you are staying in a modest hotel with a small staff, a **travel alarm** can be useful in case you need to get up early for an excursion. Small packets of **facial tissue** are a good idea because many small restaurants run out of toilet paper. Also take along lots of **suntan lotion** and **sunscreen**; prices in Acapulco are high. Bring a supply of **film**—the selection is limited and expensive. Bring plenty of **reading matter**; the selection of English-language books is limited and prices are higher than in the United States. Bring **sneakers, sandals,** and **shoes.** Mexican sizes are smaller and wider than U.S. sizes, and choice is limited. Take **dental floss** since the Mexican variety comes apart in your mouth. **Sunglasses** are expensive in Acapulco and styles are limited. A **collapsible umbrella** is handy if you are traveling between May and October. A strong **change purse** will be useful for storing all those heavy Mexican coins. A **cheap tote bag** should be used on the beach so you don't risk losing your favorite purse. The electrical current is the same as in the United States, 110 volts and 60 cycles, so an **adapter** is not necessary.

Taking Money Abroad

Traveler's checks and major U.S. credit cards are accepted in Acapulco. You'll need cash for some of the smaller restaurants and shops. Although you won't get as good an exchange rate at home as in Mexico, it's wise to change a small amount of money into Mexican pesos so you won't have to face long lines at airport currency exchange booths. Most U.S. banks will convert dollars into pesos. If your local bank does not provide this service, you can exchange money through Deak International. To find the office nearest you, contact Deak International at 630 Fifth Ave., New York, NY 10011, tel. 212/635–0515.

For safety and convenience, traveler's checks are preferable to cash. The most recognized traveler's checks are those issued by American Express, Barclay's, Thomas Cook, and major commercial banks such as Citibank and Bank of America. Some banks will issue the checks free to established customers, but most charge a 1% commission fee. AAA offers free traveler's checks to its members. Buy part of the traveler's checks in small denominations for use toward the end of your trip. This will save you from having to cash a large check and ending up with more pesos than you need. You can also buy traveler's checks in Mexican pesos, a good idea if the U.S. dollar is falling and you want to lock in the current rate (although at press time this seems unlikely, since the Mexican peso has fallen steadily over the last few years and has been devalued several times). Remember to take the addresses of offices where you can get refunds for lost or stolen traveler's checks.

Banks and *casas de cambio* (literally, houses of change) are the best places to change money. Hotels and private exchange firms offer a significantly lower rate of exchange.

Receiving Money from Home

There are at least three ways to get money from home: (1) Have it sent through a large commercial bank that has a branch in Acapulco. The only drawback is that you must have an account with the bank; if not, you'll have to go through your own bank, and the process will be slower and more costly. (2) Have it sent through American Express. If you are a cardholder, you can cash a personal check or a counter check at an American Express office for up to $1,000; $200 will be in pesos and $800 in traveler's checks. There is a 1% commission on the traveler's checks. You can also receive money through an American Express MoneyGram, which enables you to obtain up to $5,000 in cash. It works this way: You call home and ask someone to go to an American Express office—or an American Express MoneyGram agent located in a retail outlet—and fill out an American Express MoneyGram. It can be paid for with cash or with any major credit card. The person making the payment is given a reference number and telephones you with that number. The American Express MoneyGram agent calls an 800 number and authorizes the transfer of funds to the American Express office or participating agency in Acapulco. In most cases, the money is available immediately on a 24-hour basis. You pick it up by showing identification and giving the reference number. Fees vary with the amount of money sent. For $300 the fee is $22; for $5,000, the fee is $150. For the American Express MoneyGram location nearest your home and to find out the Mexican locations, call 800/543–4080. You do not have to be a cardholder to use this service. (3) Have money sent through Western Union, whose U.S. number is 800/988–4726. If you have a MasterCard or Visa, you can have money sent for any amount up to your credit limit. If not, have someone take cash or a certified cashier's check to a Western Union office. The money will be delivered to a bank in Acapulco. Fees vary with the amount of money sent. For $1,000 the fee is $26; for $500, the fee is $21.

Mexican Currency

The unit of currency in Mexico is the peso. The bills come in denominations of 50,000, 20,000, 10,000, 5,000, 2,000, 1,000, and 500. Coins are 1,000, 200, 100, 50, 20, 10, 5, and 1 peso(s). At press time (mid-May) the peso was floating and changing daily, with an exchange rate of about 2,290 pesos to the U.S. dollar, 1,795 to the Canadian dollar, and 4,000 to the pound sterling. If the peso is devalued again, there is a possibility that it will also get a new name, the azteca.

What It Will Cost

The tumble of the peso means that travel anywhere in Mexico is a bargain. This is true in Acapulco, where the dollar buys more than in years past and the not-too-picky traveler can easily spend less than $30 per day for all meals, accommodations, and sightseeing. Taxis are an especially good bargain (around $2.50 for a two-mile ride). Prices are always less if you make transactions in Spanish.

Taxes A 15% sales tax (called an IVA) is added to most purchases, although some stores include it in the price *(con IVA)*. To be sure, always ask.

Sample Prices (1988)

Cup of coffee	$ .75
Bottle of beer	1.25
Milkshake	.50
Taco from street vendor	.50
Cocktails	3.00
Two-mile taxi ride	2.50

Double room (inexpensive): under $55; (moderate): $55–$95; (expensive) $95–$250; (very expensive): $250 and up.

Passports and Visas

American Passports and visas are not formally required for entry into Mexico by U.S. citizens, though a Mexican tourist card is required. They are issued free upon proof of U.S. citizenship (valid U.S. passport, birth certificate, or certified copy of a birth certificate). Tourist cards may be obtained from Mexican consulates, the Mexican Government Tourism Office, Mexican Immigration Offices at entry points, most airlines serving Mexico, or a travel agent.

Canadian Canadian citizens need only their provincial birth certificate and a Mexican tourist card (see above).

British *See* Tips for British Travelers.

Customs and Duties

On Arrival You are allowed to take into Mexico duty-free: 400 cigarettes or 2 boxes of cigars (50 cigars); 1 still and 1 movie camera and 12 rolls of film; a reasonable amount of perfume; 3 liter bottles of liquor or wine, for personal use; prescription medicines, also for personal use; and gift items not exceeding a combined value of $120. No plant material is allowed; permits are required for firearms, and pets require a visa (contact the Mexican Embassy for details). Before clearing Mexican Customs, air travelers must complete a baggage declaration, which is distributed on all airlines entering Mexico.

On Departure If you are taking any foreign-made equipment from home, such as cameras, it's wise to carry the original receipt with you or register it with U.S. Customs before you leave (Form 4457). Otherwise you may end up paying duty on your return. **U.S. residents** who have been out of the country for at least 48 hours may bring home duty-free up to $400 worth of foreign goods. Each member of the family, regardless of age, is entitled to the same exemption, and exemptions can be pooled. For the next $1,000 worth of goods, a flat 10% rate is assessed; duties vary with the merchandise for anything over $1,400. The exemption for travelers 21 or older can include one liter of alcohol, 100 cigars (non-Cuban), and 200 cigarettes. Only one bottle of perfume trademarked in the United States may be brought in. There is no duty on antiques or art more than 100 years old. Anything exceeding these limits will be taxed at the port of entry, and may be taxed additionally in the traveler's home state. Mexico has been designated a "developing" or GSP country, which means unlimited amounts of certain goods can be taken in duty-free; check with the U.S. Customs Service, Box 7407, Washington, DC 20044. Gifts valued at less than $50 may be mailed duty-free to friends or relatives at home, but not more than one package per day to any one addressee and not to include tobacco or liquor, or perfumes costing more than $5.

Canadian residents have a $300 exemption and may also take in duty-free up to 50 cigars, 200 cigarettes, 2 pounds of tobacco, and 40 ounces of liquor, provided these are declared in writing to customs officials on arrival and accompany the traveler in hand or checked-through baggage. It is best to mail personal gifts as "Unsolicited Gift—Value under $40." Request the Canadian Customs brochure "I Declare" for further details.

British residents should consult Tips for British Travelers for reentry requirements.

Tips for British Travelers

Passports and Visas British subjects need a valid passport and a Mexican tourist card. Passports may be secured from the Passport Office in London or the branch offices in Glasgow, Liverpool, Newport, and Peterborough, or from any British consulate abroad. It costs £15 and is valid for 10 years. A Mexican tourist card may be secured from the Mexican Embassy (8 Halkin St., London SW1) or from your travel agent; or, if you are already abroad, from any Mexican Embassy or national airline office. Business travelers and students wishing to study in Mexico must inquire at the consulate for additional requirements. Passport or other proof of citizenship must be presented to reenter Great Britain.

Customs You are allowed to take into Mexico duty-free: 400 cigarettes or 2 boxes of cigars (50 cigars); 1 still and 1 movie camera and 12 rolls of film; a reasonable amount of perfume; 3 liter bottles of liquor or wine, for personal use; prescription medicines, also for personal use; and gift items not exceeding a combined value of $120. No plant material is allowed. Permits are required for firearms, and pets require a visa (contact the Mexican Embassy for details). Before clearing Mexican Customs, air travelers must complete a baggage declaration, which is distributed on all airlines entering Mexico. On your return to Britain you may bring home: (1) 200 cigarettes or 100 cigarillos or 50 cigars or 250 grams of tobacco; (2) two liters of table wine with additional allowances for (a) one liter of alcohol over 22% by volume (38.8° proof, most spirits), (b) two liters of alcohol under 22% by volume, or (c) two more liters of table wine; (3) 50 grams of perfume and 1/4 liter of toilet water; and (4) other goods up to a value of £32.

Insurance   We recommend that to cover health and motoring mishaps you insure yourself. *Europ Assistance*, 252 High St., Croydon, Surrey CRO 1NF, tel. 01/680–1234. It is also wise to take out insurance to cover loss of luggage (check, though, that this isn't already covered in an existing homeowner's policy). Trip-cancellation insurance is another wise buy. *The Association of British Insurers* (Aldermary House, Queen St., London EC4N 1TT, tel. 01/248–4477) gives comprehensive advice on all aspects of vacation insurance.

Tour Operators   Companies offering packages to Acapulco and other parts of Mexico include:

Kuoni Travel (33 Maddox St., London W1R 9LD, tel. 01/499–8636) features seven nights in Acapulco from £685, and "Mexican Highlights," a seven-night tour of Acapulco, Taxco, and Mexico City from £483.

Mexican Holidays (23 Eccleston St., London SW1 9LX, tel. 01/730–8640) can custom design an itinerary to any part of Mexico.

Thomson Holidays Ltd. (Greater London House, Hampstead Rd., London NW1 7SD, tel. 01/387–8484) offers 8-, 12-, or 15-day tours with stops in Mexico City, Taxco, and Acapulco. Thomson also has 14- and 21-day tours of classical Mexico, which include several days at a beach resort. Prices from £992–£1,339.

Electricity   Usually 110 volts; it will be helpful to bring an adapter, because appliance outlets are primarily American-style and take flat, two-pronged plugs.

Traveling with Film

If your camera is new, shoot and develop a few rolls of film before leaving home. Pack some lens tissue, and don't forget an extra battery for your built-in light meter. Invest about $10 in a skylight filter and screw it onto the front of your lens. It will protect the lens and also reduce haze.

Film doesn't like hot weather. In summer, don't store film in a car glove compartment or on the shelf under the rear window; put it behind the front seat on the floor, on the side opposite the exhaust pipe.

On a plane trip, never pack unprocessed film in check-in luggage; if your bags get X-rayed, you can say good-bye to your pictures. Always carry undeveloped film with you through security checks, and ask to have it inspected by hand. (It helps to isolate your film in a plastic bag, so it's ready for quick inspection.) Inspectors at U.S. airports are required by law to honor requests for hand inspection; abroad, you'll have to depend on the kindness of strangers.

The old airport scanning machines—still in use in some Third World countries—use heavy doses of radiation that can turn a family portrait into an early morning fog. The newer models—used in all U.S. airports—are safe for anything from five to 500 scans, depending on the speed of your film. The effects are cumulative; you can put the same roll of film through several scans without worry. After five scans, though, you're asking for trouble.

If your film gets fogged and you want an explanation, send it to the National Association of Photographic Manufacturers, 600 Mamaroneck Ave., Harrison, NY 10528. NAPM representatives will try to determine what went wrong. The service is free.

Language

English is more prevalent in Acapulco than in less touristy parts of Mexico. Hotel and restaurant staffs, taxi drivers, store clerks, and most street vendors speak English, but they will appreciate any attempt to converse with them in their native tongue. Those who speak Spanish are generally charged less by taxi drivers and vendors.

Staying Healthy

Many visitors to Mexico are eventually hit with a diarrheal intestinal ailment. Although uncomfortable, it generally is not serious and disappears in three or four days without medication. The Centers for Disease Control (CDC) in Atlanta reports that malaria exists in the Acapulco area although the risk to visitors staying in resort hotels is low.

The CDC recommends swimming in chlorinated swimming pools only—unless you are absolutely certain that the beaches and freshwater lakes are not polluted. If you are fair-skinned be sure to bring sun-screen with a high SPF factor (10 and above).

If you have a health problem that might require purchasing a prescription drug while in Mexico, have your doctor write a prescription using the drug's generic name. Brand names vary widely from country to country.

The *International Association for Medical Assistance to Travelers (IAMAT)* is a worldwide association offering a list of approved, English-speaking doctors whose training meets U.S. standards. For a list of Mexican physicians and clinics that are part of this network, contact IAMAT, 736 Center St., Lewiston, NY 14092. In Canada: 188 Nicklin Rd., Guelph, Ontario, N1H 7L5. In Europe: Gotthardstrasse 17, 6300 Zug, Switzerland. Membership is free.

Shots and Medications The American Medical Association (AMA) recommends Pepto-Bismol for traveler's diarrhea. The CDC recommends malaria-preventive drugs if you plan to go off the beaten path. Because malaria is carried by a mosquito that feeds at night, be certain your hotel room has screens, spray yourself liberally with insect repellent after sunset, and wear protective clothing.

Persons entering Mexico from areas infected with yellow fever must have a certificate of vaccination. For a list of those areas, contact your local health department or the nearest Mexican consulate.

Insurance

Travelers may seek insurance coverage in three areas: health and accident, loss of luggage, and trip cancellation. Your first step is to review your existing health and homeowner policies; some health insurance plans cover health expenses incurred while traveling, some major medical plans cover emergency transportation, and some homeowner policies cover the theft of luggage.

Health and Accident Several companies offer coverage designed to supplement existing health insurance for travelers:

Carefree Travel Insurance (Box 310, 120 Mineola Blvd., Mineola, NY 11501, tel. 800/645–2424 or 516/294–0220) provides coverage for medical evacuation. It also offers 24-hour medical advice by phone.

Health Care Abroad, International Underwriters Group (243 Church St. West, Vienna, VA 22180, tel. 800/237–6615 or 703/281–9500), offers comprehensive medical coverage, including emergency evacuation, for trips of 10 to 90 days.

International SOS Insurance (Box 11568, Philadelphia, PA 19116, tel. 800/523–8930 or 215/244–1500) does not provide medical insurance but makes medical evacuation available to its clients, who are often international corporations.

Travel Guard International, (1100 Centerpoint Dr., Stevens Point, WI 54481, tel. 800/782–5151 or 715/345–0505), underwritten by Cygna, offers medical insurance, with coverage for emergency evacuation when Travel Guard's representatives in the United States say it is necessary.

Loss of Luggage Luggage loss coverage is usually part of a comprehensive travel insurance package that includes personal accident, trip cancellation, and sometimes default and bankruptcy. Several companies offer broad policies:

Access America Inc., a subsidiary of Blue Cross-Blue Shield, Box 807, New York, NY 10163, tel. 800/851–2800.

Near, Inc., 1900 N. MacArthur Blvd., Suite 210, Oklahoma City, OK 73127, tel. 800/654–6700.

Travel Guard International *(See* Health and Accident Insurance).

Trip Cancellation Flight insurance is often included in the price of a ticket when purchased with American Express, Visa, or another major credit card. It is usually included in travel insurance packages available from many tour operators, travel agents, and insurance agents.

Car Rentals

If you're flying into Acapulco and plan to spend some time there, save money by arranging to pick up your car in town the day you need it; otherwise, arrange to pick up and return your car at the airport. You'll have to weigh the added expense of renting a car from a major company with an airport office against the savings on a car from a budget company with offices in town. You could waste precious hours trying to locate the budget company in return for only a small saving. Be prepared to pay more for a car with an automatic transmission and since they are not readily available, reserve them in advance. Rental rates vary widely, depending on size and model, number of days you use the car, insurance coverage, and whether special drop-off fees are imposed. In most cases, rates quoted include unlimited free mileage and standard liability protection. Collision damage waiver (CDW), which eliminates your deductible should you have an accident, is mandatory in Mexico. Not included are personal accident insurance, gasoline, and a local 15% sales tax.

You must be 21 or older to drive a car in Mexico. Driver's licenses issued in the United States and Canada are valid. You might also take out an International Driving Permit before you leave, not only to smooth out difficulties if you have an accident but also to serve as an additional piece of identification should you need it. Permits are available for a small fee through local offices of the American Automobile Association (AAA) and the Canadian Automobile Association (CAA), or from their main offices: AAA, 8111 Gatehouse Rd., Falls Church, VA 22047, tel. 703/AAA–6000; or CAA, 2 Carlton St., Toronto, Ontario M5B 1K4, tel. 416/964–3170.

It's best to arrange a car rental before you leave. You won't save money by waiting until you arrive in Acapulco, and you may find that the type of car you want is not available at the last minute. Rental companies usually charge according to the exchange rate of the dollar at the time the car is returned or when the credit card payment is processed. Companies that serve Acapulco include **Budget Rent-a-Car** (tel. 800/527–0700), **Avis** (tel. 800/331–1212), **Hertz**, (tel. 800/223–6472; in NY, 800/522–5568), and **National** (tel. 800/CAR–RENT).

Student and Youth Travel

The **International Student Identity Card (ISIC)** entitles students to youth rail passes, special fares on local transportation, and discounts at museums, theaters, sports events, and many other attractions. If purchased in the United States, the $10 cost of the ISIC also includes $2,000 in emergency medical insurance, plus $100 a day for up to 60 days of hospital coverage. Apply to the Council on International Educational Exchange (CIEE), 205 E. 42nd St., New York, NY 10017, tel. 212/661–1414. In Canada, the ISIC is available from the Federation of Students—Services, 187 College St., Toronto, Ontario M5T 1P7, for CN$10.

Council Travel, a CIEE subsidiary, is the foremost U.S. student travel agency, specializing in low-cost charters and serving as the exclusive U.S. agent for many student airfare bargains and student tours. (CIEE's 80-page *Student Travel Catalog* and "Council Charter" brochure are available free from any Council Travel office in the U.S. (enclose $1 postage if ordering by mail). In addition to the CIEE headquarters at 205 East 42nd Street and a branch office at 35 West 8th Street in New York City, there are Council Travel offices in Amherst, Austin, Berkeley, Boston, Cambridge, Chicago, Dallas, La

Jolla, Long Beach, Los Angeles, Portland, Providence, San Diego, San Francisco, and Seattle.

The **Educational Travel Center,** another student travel specialist worth contacting for information on student tours, bargain fares, and bookings, may be reached at 438 N. Frances St., Madison, WI 55703, tel. 608/256–5551.

Students who would like to work abroad should contact *CIEE's Work Abroad Department* (at 205 E. 42nd St., New York, NY 10017). The council arranges various types of paid and voluntary work experiences overseas for up to six months. CIEE also sponsors study programs in Latin America, Asia, and publishes many books of interest to the student traveler: These include *Work, Study, Travel Abroad: The Whole World Handbook* ($8.95 plus $1 postage); *Work Your Way Around the World* ($10.95 plus $1 postage); and *Volunteer! The Comprehensive Guide to Voluntary Service in the U.S. and Abroad* ($5.50 plus $1 postage).

The Information Center at the **Institute of International Education,** IIE (809 UN Plaza, New York, NY 10017, tel. 212/984–5413), has reference books, foreign university catalogues, study-abroad brochures, and other materials, which may be consulted by students and nonstudents alike, free of charge. The Information Center is open from 10 to 4, Mon.–Fri., and until 7 Wed.

IIE administers a variety of grant and study programs offered by U.S. and foreign organizations, and publishes a well-known annual series of study-abroad guides, including *Academic Year Abroad, Vacation Study Abroad,* and *Study in the United Kingdom and Ireland.* The institute also publishes *Teaching Abroad,* a book of employment and study opportunities overseas for U.S. teachers. For a current list of IIE publications, prices and ordering information, write to Publications Service, Institute of International Education, 809 UN Plaza, New York, NY 10017. Books must be purchased by mail or in person; telephone orders are not accepted.

General information on IIE programs and services is available from its regional offices in Atlanta, Chicago, Denver, Houston, San Francisco, and Washington, DC.

Traveling with Children

Publications   *Family Travel Times,* an 8- or 12-page newsletter published 10 times a year by TWYCH (Travel with Your Children, 80 Eighth Ave., New York, NY 10011, tel. 212/206–0688). Subscription includes access to back issues and twice-weekly opportunities to call in for specific information.

Villa Rentals   **At Home Abroad, Inc.,** 405 E. 56th St., Suite 6H, New York, NY 10022, tel. 212/421–9165. **Villas International,** 71 W. 23rd St., New York, NY 10010, tel. 800/221–2260; 212/929–7585. **Hideaways, Inc.,** Box 1464, Littleton, MA 01460, tel. 617/486–8955. **Villas and Apartments Abroad,** 444 Madison Ave., Suite 211, New York, NY 10022, tel. 212/759–1025.

Home Exchange   See *Home Exchanging: A Complete Sourcebook for Travelers at Home or Abroad* by James Dearing (Globe Pequot Press, Box Q, Chester, CT 06412, tel. 800/243–0495; in CT 800/962–0973).

Getting There On international flights, children under two not occupying a seat pay 10% of adult fare. Various discounts apply to children 2–12. Reserve a seat behind the bulkhead of the plane, which offers more leg room and can usually fit a bassinet (supplied by the airline). At the same time, inquire about special children's meals or snacks, offered by most airlines. (See "TWYCH's Airline Guide," in the February 1988 issue of *Family Travel Times*, for a rundown on children's services furnished by 46 airlines.) Ask your airline in advance if you can bring aboard your child's car seat. (For the booklet "Child/Infant Safety Seats Acceptable for Use in Aircraft," write Community and Consumer Liaison Division, APA-400 Federal Aviation Administration, Washington, DC 20591, tel. 202/267–3479.)

Baby-sitting Child-care arrangements are easily made through your hotel **Services** concierge.

Hints for Disabled Travelers

The **Information Center for Individuals with Disabilities** (20 Park Plaza, Room 330, Boston, MA 02116, tel. 617/727–5540) offers useful problem-solving assistance, including lists of travel agents who specialize in tours for the disabled.

Moss Rehabilitation Hospital Travel Information Service (12th St. and Tabor Rd., Philadelphia, PA 19141, tel. 215/329–5715) provides information on tourist sights, transportation, and accommodations in destinations around the world. The fee is $5 for each destination. Allow one month for delivery.

Mobility International (Box 3551, Eugene, OR 97403, tel. 503/343–1284) has information on accommodations, organized study, and so forth, around the world.

The **Society for the Advancement of Travel for the Handicapped** (26 Court St., Penthouse Suite, Brooklyn, NY 11242, tel. 718/858–5483) offers access information. Annual membership is $40, or $25 for senior travelers and students. Send $1 and a stamped, self-addressed envelope.

The Itinerary (Box 1084, Bayonne, NJ 07002, tel. 201/858–3400) is a bimonthly travel magazine for the disabled.

Access to the World: A Travel Guide for the Handicapped by Louise Weiss is useful but out of date. Available from the publisher, Henry Holt & Co., tel. 212/599–7600.

Frommer's Guide for Disabled Travelers is also useful but dated.

Hints for Older Travelers

The **American Association of Retired Persons** (AARP, 1909 K St. NW, Washington, DC 20049, tel. 202/662–4850) has two programs for independent travelers: (1) the Purchase Privilege Program, which offers discounts on hotels, airfare, car rentals, and sightseeing; and (2) the AARP Motoring Plan, which furnishes emergency aid and trip routing information for an annual fee of $29.95 per couple. AARP members must be 50 or older. Annual dues are $5 per person or per couple.

To use an AARP or other identification card, ask for a reduced hotel rate at the time you make your reservation rather than when you check out. At restaurants, show your card to the maître d' before you're seated, because discounts may be limited to certain set menus, days, or hours. When renting a car, remember that economy cars, priced at promotional rates, may cost less than cars that are available with your ID card.

Travel Industry and Disabled Exchange (TIDE, 5435 Donna Ave., Tarzana, CA 91356, tel. 818/343–6339) is an industry-based organization with a $15 per person annual membership fee. Members receive a quarterly newsletter and information on travel agencies and tours.

National Council of Senior Citizens (925 15th St. NW, Washington, DC 20005, tel. 202/347–8800) is a nonprofit advocacy group with some 4,000 local clubs across the country. Annual membership is $10 per person or $14 per couple. Members receive a monthly newspaper with travel information and an ID card for reduced-rate hotels and car rentals.

Mature Outlook (Box 1205, Glenview, IL 60025, tel. 800/336–6330), a subsidiary of Sears, Roebuck & Co., is a travel club for people over 50, with hotel and motel discounts and a bimonthly newsletter. Annual membership is $7.50 per couple. Instant membership is available at participating Holiday Inns.

Travel Tips for Senior Citizens (U.S. Dept. of State Publication 8970, revised September 1987) is available for $1 from the Superintendant of Documents, U.S. Government Printing Office, Washington, DC 20402.

Getting to Acapulco

From the North by Plane

There are three types of flights to Acapulco: nonstop—no changes, no stops; direct—no changes but one or more stops; and connecting—two or more planes, one or more stops.

The Airlines From the United States: **American** (tel. 800/433–7300) has nonstops from Chicago and Dallas; connections from New York through Dallas. **Continental** (tel. 800/525–0280) has nonstops from Atlanta and Houston and Newark airport (Saturdays only). **Delta's** (tel. 800/843–9378) nonstop service is from Atlanta, Dallas, and Los Angeles. **Mexicana** (tel. 800/531–7921) has nonstops from Chicago, Dallas, Denver, Los Angeles, Philadelphia, San Antonio, San Francisco, and Seattle, connecting service from Baltimore, Miami, and Tampa. Other major carriers such as **Pan Am** fly into Mexico City, where you can make a connection to Acapulco.

From Canada: **Delta** has flights from most major Canadian cities via Los Angeles to Acapulco; **Japan Air** (tel. 800/525–3663) flies from Vancouver nonstop into Mexico City, where connections are available into Acapulco; **Ward Air** (tel. 800/387–7667) has nonstop charter flights from Toronto to Acapulco.

Flying Time From New York via Dallas, 4 1/2 hours; from Chicago, 4 1/4 hours; from Los Angeles, 3 1/2 hours.

Luggage Regulations *Checked Luggage* U.S. airlines allow passengers to check in two suitcases whose total dimensions (length + width + height) do not exceed 60 inches. There are no weight restrictions on these bags.

Rules governing foreign airlines vary from airline to airline, so check with your travel agent or the airline itself before you go. All airlines allow passengers to check in two bags. In general, expect the weight restriction on the two bags to be not more than 70 pounds each, and the size restriction on the first bag to be 62 inches total dimensions, and on the second bag, 55 inches total dimensions.

Carry-on Luggage   New rules have been in effect since January 1, 1988, on U.S. airlines with regard to carry-on luggage. The model for these new rules was agreed to by the airlines in December 1987 and then circulated by the Air Transport Association with the understanding that each airline would present its own version.

Under the model, passengers are limited to two carry-on bags. For a bag you wish to store under the seat, the maximum dimensions are 9″ x 14″ x 22″, a total of 45″. For bags that can be hung in a closet or on a luggage rack, the maximum dimensions are 4″ x 23″ x 45″, a total of 72″. For bags you wish to store in an overhead bin, the maximum dimensions are 10″ x 14″ x 36″, a total of 60″. Your two carry-ons must each fit one of these sets of dimensions, and any item that exceeds the specified dimensions will generally be rejected as a carry-on, and handled as checked baggage. Keep in mind that an airline can adapt these rules to circumstances, so on an especially crowded flight, don't be surprised if you are allowed only one carry-on bag.

In addition to the two carry-ons, the rules list eight items that may also be brought aboard: a handbag (pocketbook or purse), an overcoat or wrap, an umbrella, a camera, a reasonable amount of reading material, an infant bag, crutches, cane, braces, or other prosthetic device upon which the passenger is dependent, and an infant/child safety seat.

Note that these regulations are for U.S. airlines only. Foreign airlines generally allow one piece of carry-on luggage in tourist class, in addition to handbags and bags filled with duty-free goods. It is best to check with your airline ahead of time to find out the exact rules regarding carry-on luggage.

Luggage Insurance   Airlines are responsible for lost or damaged property only up to $1,250 per passenger on domestic flights, and $9.07 per pound (or $20 per kilo) for checked baggage on international flights, and up to $400 per passenger for unchecked baggage on international flights. If you're carrying valuables, either take them with you on the airplane or purchase additional insurance for lost luggage. Some airlines will issue additional luggage insurance when you check in, but many do not. One that does is American Airlines. Its additional insurance is only for domestic flights or flights to Canada. Rates are $1 for every $100 valuation, with a maximum of $400 valuation per passenger. Hand luggage is not included. Insurance for lost, damaged, or stolen luggage is available through travel agents or directly through various insurance companies. Two that issue luggage insurance are **Tele-Trip** (tel. 800/228–9792), a subsidiary of Mutual of Omaha, and the **Travelers Insurance Co.** (tel. 800/243–0191). Tele-Trip operates sales booths at airports, and also issues insurance through travel agents. Tele-Trip will insure checked luggage for up to 180 days and for $500 to $3,000 valuation. For 1–3 days, the rate for a $500 valuation is $8.25;

for 180 days, $100. The Travelers Insurance Co. will insure checked or hand luggage for $500–$2,000 valuation per person, and also for a maximum of 180 days. Rates for 1–5 days for $500 valuation are $10; for 180 days, $85. For more information, write the Travelers Insurance Co., Ticket and Travel Dept., 1 Tower Sq., Hartford, CT 06183. Both companies offer the same rates on domestic and international flights. Check the travel pages of your Sunday newspaper for the names of other companies that insure luggage. Before you go, itemize the contents of each bag in case you need to file an insurance claim. Be certain to put your address on each piece of luggage, including carry-on bags. (A business address is recommended, so thieves don't have directions to your empty house.) If your luggage is stolen and later recovered, the airline must deliver the luggage to your home free of charge.

Discount Flights The major airlines offer a range of tickets that can increase the price of any given seat by more than 300%, depending on the day of purchase. As a rule, the further in advance you buy the ticket, the less expensive it is and the greater the penalty (up to 100%) for canceling. Check with airlines for details.

It's important to distinguish between companies that sell seats on charter flights and companies that sell one of a block of tickets on scheduled airlines. Charter flights are the least expensive and the least reliable—with chronically late departures and not infrequent cancellations. They also tend to depart less frequently (usually once a week) than regularly scheduled flights. A wise alternative to a charter is a ticket on a scheduled flight purchased from a wholesaler or ticket broker. It's an unbeatable deal: a scheduled flight at up to 50% off the APEX fare. Tickets can usually be purchased up to three days before departure (but in high season expect to wait in line an hour or so).

The following brokers specialize in discount sales; all charge an annual fee of about $35–$50. **Discount Travel International** (114 Forrest Ave., Narberth, PA 19072, tel. 800/458–0503), **Moment's Notice** (40 E. 49th St., New York, NY 10017, tel. 212/486–0503); **Stand-Buys Ltd.,** (311 W. Superior, Suite 414, Chicago, IL 60610, tel. 800/255–0200), **Worldwide Discount Travel Club,** (1674 Meridian Ave., Miami Beach, FL 33139, tel. 305/534–2082).

Enjoying the Flight If you're lucky to be able to sleep on a plane, it makes sense to fly at night. Unless you are flying from Europe or Great Britain, jet lag won't be a problem. There is little or no time difference between Acapulco and the United States and Canada. Sleepers usually prefer window seats to curl up against; those who like to move about the cabin should request an aisle seat. Bulkhead seats (adjacent to the "Exit" signs) have more leg room, but seat trays are attached rather awkwardly to the arms of your seat rather than to the back of the seat ahead.

Smoking If smoking bothers you, ask for a seat far away from the smoking section. If the airline tells you there are no nonsmoking seats, insist on one: Department of Transportation regulations require airlines to find seats for all nonsmokers.

From the Airport to Center City Private taxis are not permitted to carry passengers from the airport to town, so most people rely on buses, sedans, or combis (minibuses). The system looks confusing but it's not, and there are dozens of helpful English-speaking staff to help you figure out which bus to take.

● Look for the name of your hotel and the number of its zone on the overhead sign on the walkway in front of the terminal.

● Go to the desk for your zone and buy a ticket for either a bus or a combi (minibus) that goes to your zone. Each costs about $5. The drivers are usually helpful and will often take you to hotels not on their list. Tips are optional.

● At one end of the car rental desk it is sometimes possible to rent a sedan for about $20 or a limousine for $30. The journey into town takes from 20 to 30 minutes. Whichever way you travel, buy only a one-way ticket because taxis to the airport are inexpensive.

From the North by Car

A car can be handy in Acapulco, but we don't recommend you drive from either the United States or Canada. Except for major highways, the roads are not well maintained and distances from the border are great (at least 16 hours from Laredo to Mexico City and another six from there to Acapulco). If you prefer to see the sights by car, we suggest renting a car once you're in Acapulco (*see* Renting Cars in Before You Go).

Whether you drive from the United States or Canada or rent a car in Acapulco, bear in mind that Mexico is a developing country and things are much different than in North America or Western Europe.

The biggest problem at this writing is finding unleaded gasoline. Since the September 1985 earthquakes, promises have been made to correct the situation, but drivers should check with an auto club to find out if the promises have been kept.

Spare parts are another worry. Parts for a Ford or Chevy are plentiful, but getting a new transmission for a Toyota or Mercedes is not easy.

The best highway, although two lanes most of the way, is Route 85 from Laredo to Monterrey and Route 57 on to Mexico City. Driving time is about 16 hours.

The trip to Acapulco from Mexico City takes about six hours, but many people opt for going via Taxco and spending at least one night there.

Practical Tips There are two absolutely essential things to remember about driving in Mexico. First and foremost is to carry insurance. If you injure anyone in an accident, you could well be jailed— whether it was your fault or not—unless you have insurance. This is part of the country's Napoleon Code: guilty until proven innocent.

The second item is that if you enter Mexico with a car, you must leave with it. The fact that you drove in with a car is stamped on your tourist card, which you must give to immigration authorities at departure. If an emergency arises and you must fly home, there are complicated procedures to face with customs.

The reason is that cars are much cheaper in the United States, and you are not allowed to sell your vehicle in Mexico. The authorities at the airport assume that, unless you have a customs release, you have sold your car for a hefty profit. If such a situation should arise, contact the customs officials at the airport to see if you may leave your car in their special parking lot.

Mileage and speed limits are given in kilometers; 100 kph and 80 kph (62 and 50 mph, respectively) are the most common maximum speeds. A few of the newer toll roads allow 110 kph (68.4 mph). Cities and towns may have posted speed limits of 40 kph (25 mph), sometimes even 30 kph (18 mph), and it's best to observe them. (See Appendix I for metric conversion tables.)

Streets in Acapulco can be one- or two-way. Your guide is an arrow posted on the sides of corner buildings, its point indicating the direction of traffic flow. A two-pointed arrow means two-way traffic. The arrow may have the words *tránsito* or *circulación* printed on it.

In town, a sign with a large *E* inside a circle stands for *estacionamiento*, or parking. Much more frequently seen is the same sign with a strong bar diagonally through the *E* and maybe the word *NO* underneath—no parking!

When you approach one end of a narrow bridge *(puente angosto)* at the same time that another car approaches the opposite end, the first one to flick his lights has the right of way.

Don't drive at night unless absolutely necessary, and even then only on the superhighways. The hazards are too many—you can't see roaming animals soon enough; large rocks may have been left on the pavement by some motorist who had car trouble and braced his wheels with them; a pedestrian or cyclist appears around a sudden curve; new rock slides occur in mountain areas during the rainy season; potholes abound—the list is a long one and the risk not worth the mileage gained.

During the day be alert to cattle crossings. Free-grazing animals may decide to amble across the highway just as you approach. Domestic animals frequently graze along the shoulders, and the sight or sound of an approaching car could cause one or more to bolt—not always away from the pavement. Older animals are wise to the dangers of the highway and will seldom move fast, but watch for the young ones, like calves. They're nervous and easily frightened into bolting.

There are several toll roads in Mexico, covering mostly the last stretches of major highways leading to the capital. Some of these roads are two-lane affairs but most are four-lane with a divider strip. These highways have toll-free roads running roughly parallel to them. The toll roads have signs that say *cuota* and give the destination (usually *México*, meaning Mexico City, and perhaps an intermediary city) while the parallel routes have signs saying *libre* (free) with the destination. These two signs, with arrows pointing in different directions, are usually posted before the road splits. Remember that because of the mountainous nature of central and southern Mexico and the many trucks on the highways, driving times are longer than for comparable distances in the United States. There are also toll bridges in various parts of the country.

When you buy insurance, you will probably receive a folder showing Mexican road signs. Here are a few words on the road signs that you should know: *alto*—stop; *no rebase*—do not pass; *ceda el paso*—yield right of way; *conserve su derecha* —keep to the right; *curva peligrosa*—dangerous curve; *derrumbes*—landslide zone; *despacio* (sometimes also *disminuya su velocidad*)—slow down; *tramo en reparación*— road work ahead; *puente angosto*—narrow bridge; *no hay paso* —road closed; *desviación*—detour.

Topes, meaning bumps, are indicated by a sign showing a series of bumps. As many highways—sometimes even major ones— cut through towns and villages, these bumps are the only way to slow down the speeding traffic to protect life and livestock. Take it easy when approaching any village—at times the bumps are there but the signs are not.

As you climb into the highlands of central Mexico, your car might not feel quite right because of the altitude. This could be a result of the lower-octane gasoline or your carburetor's needing adjustment.

Road maps are handy for those traveling by car in Mexico. A large selection of the most up-to-date maps are available from Bradt Enterprises (95 Harvey St., Cambridge, MA 02140, tel. 617/492–8776). In Mexico, try Guía Roji's *Atlas de Carreteras*.

Aid to Motorists **The "Green Angels."** The Mexican Tourism Secretariat operates a fleet of about 230 special pickup trucks on all the nation's major highways to render assistance to motorists. Though known officially as the *Tourist Assistance Service*, everyone calls them with affection, the *Green Angels*. The bilingual drivers are equipped to offer mechanical first aid to your car, medical first aid to you, communication through a two-way radio-telephone network, basic supplies of all types, towing if needed, adjustment and changing of tires, tourist information, and protection. The trucks are painted two shades of green and have a flashing red light atop the cab. The doors carry printed identification in English and Spanish. The number of Green Angels has been increased in recent years.

How to hail one in case of need? Pull off the road as far as possible and lift the hood of your car. If you're on an isolated section of highway, hail the first passing car in either direction and ask the driver to notify the patrol of your trouble. Bus drivers and drivers of heavy trucks will also be helpful in this respect.

The patrol's services are rendered free of charge. Tips, however, are not refused. Spare parts, fuel, and lubricants are provided at cost.

The Green Angels patrol fixed sections of highway, passing a given spot several times a day. The service is provided from 8 AM to around 8 PM every day on major highways.

Insurance Remember that your foreign car insurance coverage is no good in Mexico. Purchase enough Mexican automobile insurance at the border to cover the length of your trip. It's sold by the day, and if your trip is shorter than your original estimate, a prorated refund for the unused time will be issued to you upon application after you exit the country. *Dan Sanborn's Insurance* and *Seguros Atlántico* (Allstate reps) have offices in most border cities. Also, you might try *Instant Mexico Auto Insurance*, San Ysidro and Chula Vista, CA, and Nogales, AZ. All three are experienced and reliable.

Always lock your car securely in Mexico when no one's in it. *Never* leave valuable items in the body of the car; either lock them in the trunk or carry them with you into your hotel or motel at night.

Service Stations Your American gasoline charge cards won't work in Mexico. All service stations are *Pemex*—the national gas company. Stations are fairly few and far between. Always fill up once the gauge hits the half-empty mark.

Regular gasoline, around 80 octane, was selling for U.S. 75 cents a gallon at press time. Regular gas is sold out of blue pumps. When available, nonleaded Extra, around 90 octane, is sold out of silver-colored pumps. It was going for 120 pesos a liter or roughly 95 cents a gallon. (The red pumps are for diesel fuel.) Pumps measure gas not by the gallon but by the liter. (*See* Appendix 1 for metric conversion tables).

Oil: Pemex's *Faja de Oro* (black and gold can), *Esso, Shell, Quaker State,* and *Mobiloil* are best grades of motor oil. Pemex products usually cost less. Mexican-made tires are of good quality but are more expensive than in the U.S. and Canada.

Rest rooms have been modernized, and are periodically inspected for cleanliness and serviceability. In between inspections, however, some station operators neglect them, while others, to assure their proper maintenance, keep them under lock and key. If you must ask for the key to a locked ladies room, say *"la llave para damas, por favor"* (la YAH-vay pah-rah DAH-mahs, pohr fah-VOHR) for a men's room key, say *"caballeros"* (cah-bah-YEHR-ohs).

Tell the attendant *"Lleno, por favor"* (YAY-noh)—that is, "Fill'er up." Point out the pump you want. Most cars do well on the *Nova* (blue pump), but if yours is a late U.S. model, you'll need the *Extra* (unleaded, in silver pump). Check to be sure the pump gauge is turned back to zero before the attendant starts pumping your gas; as soon as the tank is filled, write down the amount of pesos shown as due. In a busy station—and most highway stations are—a second attendant may turn the gauge back to zero to service another car and your amount due may be forgotten (or escalated). Write it down to be on the safe side.

A tip, the equivalent of a quarter or so for extra services, such as having your windshield cleaned or your oil checked, is customary and expected. The gas stations do not have mechanics.

Automobile Repair You may have heard tales about how Mexican mechanics put motors back together with bobby pins and glue. True, many mechanics are resourceful and capable, as evidenced by the large numbers of vintage automobiles still plying the streets. However, finding U.S.-made spare parts can be a major problem, as is trying to locate an English-speaking mechanic. We suggest that you ask for help at your hotel if you need mechanical work done on your car.

Parking We suggest parking in pay lots, usually called *estacionamiento* (parking), as towing away illegally parked cars is becoming common.

Missing License Plates Mexican police have always employed a most effective means for punishing those who park their automobiles in prohibited areas—they remove one license plate. Redeeming it requires a trip to the local *tránsito* headquarters and the payment of a fine.

Witnessing an Accident When you see an accident or an injured person, think twice before stopping to help. As a rule, it is best to notify the first policeman you see or, if on the highway, the first Green Angel Tourism Secretariat truck or highway patrol car. Not helping an injured person may be contrary to your instincts and training, but it can get you seriously involved, even thrown in jail. You can be accused of *mal medicina*, for instance, if you move an injured person. He, or the police, can later charge that you made things worse. If he dies you could even be implicated in the death.

Police The color and cut of police uniforms vary throughout the Mexican Republic. Mexico City traffic and civil police all wear blue uniforms—with the addition of white gloves for dress occasions.

From the North by Ship

Many cruises include Acapulco as part of their itinerary. Most originate from Los Angeles. Cruise operators include: *Carnival Cruise Lines* (tel. 800/327–9051); *Holland American Lines* (tel. 800/426–0327); *Princess Cruises* (tel. 800/421–0522); *Royal Viking Line* (tel. 800/233–8000); *Sitmar Cruises* (tel. 800/421–0880). Bookings are generally handled through a travel agent.

For details on freighter travel to or from Mexico, consult *Pearl's Freighter Tips*, 175 Great Neck Rd., Great Neck, NY 11021, tel. 516/487–8351.

From the North by Train and Bus

There is no train service to Acapulco from anywhere in the United States or Canada. Buses to Acapulco can be boarded on the U.S. side of the border, but the trip is not recommended; even the most experienced travelers find the trip exhausting and uncomfortable. Bus service from Mexico City to Acapulco however, is worth trying, especially if you want to see some of the Mexican countryside. Buses are comfortable and in good condition and the trip takes six hours. They leave three times a day from Tasqueña station. A first-class ticket costs $7. You check your baggage and collect it from the baggage window at the Estrella de Oro bus station in Acapulco when you arrive.

From the United Kingdom by Plane

There are no direct flights to Acapulco from the United Kingdom, though the following airlines have service via Mexico City or major United States or European cities: **Air France** (tel. 01/499–9511); **British Airways** (tel. 01/759–5511); **Iberia** (tel. 01/437–5622); **KLM** (tel. 01/568–9144). The flying time will vary depending on point of departure.

2 Portraits of Acapulco

Host to the World

by Erica Meltzer

A frequent visitor
to Mexico since
1967, Erica lived
in Mexico City for
three years. A
writer and
translator, her
specialty is
Mexico.

The story of Acapulco begins with a Romeo-and-Juliet-like myth of the Yope Indians. (This tribe had been driven to Acapulco from the north by the Nahuas, forerunners of the Aztecs.) Acatl (his name means "reed") firstborn son of the tribal chief, heard a voice telling him that in order to perpetuate his race, he should seek the love of Quiahuitl ("rain"), daughter of an enemy chieftain. Acatl went in search of Quiahuitl, and though the two fell in love, her father refused to allow the marriage. Grief-stricken, Acatl returned to his home in the foothills of the Sierra Madre above the Bay of Acapulco, intent on being devoured by the animals.

But Acatl missed the sweet warbling of the zenzontle bird and returned to the bay to lie beneath the mesquite tree. (The seed of the mesquite had been carried there by Acatl's father from their northern homeland.) The mesquite, a spiny tropical tree with roots that penetrate deep into the ground for water, is sacred to the Indians. Unable to forget Quiahuitl, Acatl wept so hard that his body dissolved into a puddle of mud, which spread across the coastal plain. From the mud sprung little reeds, yellowish green tinged with red: These were the sons of Acatl, bearing the colors of the mesquite and the zenzontle.

Quiahuitl, in turn, was transformed into an immense cloud and floated toward the bay where, finding her lost love, she dissolved in tears. The teardrops fell on the reeds, and Quiahuitl was united forever with Acatl. This is said to be the origin of the name Acapulco, which means "in the place where the reeds were destroyed." The legend holds that whenever the bay is threatened by clouds, Quiahuitl, remembering her love, will return.

Acapulco has been inhabited since at least 3000 BC; the oldest Nahua artifacts in the region date from 2,000 years ago. These artifacts—clay heads, known as the "Pretty Ladies of Acapulco"—were discovered in the lost city of La Sabana, in the hills outside Acapulco. The region boasts few other archaeological remains because of earthquakes.

From 1486 to 1502, after centuries under Toltec rule, Acapulco became part of the Aztec empire. It was then taken over by the Tarascans, another Indian tribe, along with the rest of the province of Zacatula. It was such power struggles among the Indians that eventually led to Acapulco's conquest by the Spaniards under Hernán Cortés. Montezuma II, the Aztec emperor, told Cortés that more gold came from Zacatula than from anywhere else so that Cortés would conquer Montezuma's rivals, the Tarascans.

Acapulco was discovered by Francisco Chico on December 13, 1521, and has been a magnet for seekers of wealth ever since. Chico had been sent by Cortés to find sites for ports, as Cortés was obsessed with locating a route to the Spice Islands. Acapulco has a great natural harbor, twice as deep as either San Francisco or New York, and so was a perfect choice. In accordance with a custom of Spanish explorers, Chico named the bay after the saint whose feast day coincided with the day of his landing: Santa Lucía. Cortés then built a mule path from Mexico City to Acapulco—his Spanish overlords forbade the use of Indians to transport cargo—and used the settlement to build ships for his explorations of the South Pacific. In 1532, it officially became a domain of the Spanish crown, known as the *Ciudad de los Reyes*, or City of the Kings. Cortés went frequently to Acapulco, staying at Puerto Marqués Bay, which was named for him (Cortés was the marquis, or Marqués, of the Valley of Oaxaca).

By 1579, Acapulco was booming, and King Philip II decreed it the only official port for trade between America and Asia—primarily the Philippines, which had been discovered by Spaniards sailing from Acapulco. (In the Spanish spoken in the Philippines, *acapulco* is the name of a plant, the *Cassia alata*, introduced to the Philippines by traders from Mexico.) For centuries afterward, the port played a crucial role in the history of the New World: In 1537, Cortés sent ships to Pizarro to help his conquest of Peru, and two years later, he launched an expedition to discover the Seven Cities of Cíbola. Ships from Acapulco explored Cape Mendocino, California, in 1602.

But it was the Manila galleons—the *naos de China*—which brought Acapulco its early fame. The first vessel, the *San Pablo*, sailed in 1565, and for the next 250 years the Spanish crown maintained a stranglehold on trade with the Orient. The *naos* carried the richest cargo of their day: silks, porcelain, cottons, rugs, jade, ivory, incense, spices, and slaves. Altogether, $2 million worth of goods reached Acapulco from the East. The goods were then carried overland—a 20-day journey along the six-foot-wide "Road to Asia" trail—to Veracruz on the Gulf of Mexico, where other ships then bore the cargo to Europe. On their return voyages to the East, the galleons transported silver from Mexico and Peru. The Spaniards limited the traffic to one arrival a year, usually at Christmas, and this event was heralded by the great Acapulco Fair of the Americas. Traders and merchants came from all over New Spain to buy the goods, and the malaria-ridden village, normally home to 4,000 people (mostly blacks and mulattoes), was suddenly host to 12,000.

Thus, from its early days Acapulco became well versed in the arts of hospitality. Because accommodations were insufficient to lodge the flood of visitors, locals developed a lucrative business by renting out houses, patios, corrals, and even doorways. They made fortunes as entertainers, quack doctors, porters, food vendors, and water carriers. Visitors amused themselves with bullfights, cockfights, and horse races. So much Peruvian gold and silver changed hands that the mules were literally laden down with coins, and the Spanish Crown was obliged to remint the precious metals and exploit the Mexican silver mines.

All this wealth had several unfortunate consequences for Acapulco and New Spain. One was that the monopolies enjoyed by the guilds of Acapulco and Veracruz kept prices high, and the demand for locally produced goods low. Eventually, the Spaniards allowed two overland journeys a year, and established other ports to relieve the trade bottleneck. In an attempt to benefit further from the commerce, the Spaniards instituted the first customs office in 1646, taxing all goods sold at the fair and limiting imports. The move backfired, as merchants began unloading their goods in Zihuatanejo, producing Mexico's first traffic in contraband, and eventually discouraging trade altogether, given the hazards of ocean crossings.

The other outcome was the arrival of pirates. Until Sir Francis Drake's *Golden Hind* first sailed into Acapulco Bay in his exploration of the Pacific, the riches of the Manila galleons were a Spanish secret. Drake, whose ship was shot at by panicking Spaniards, boarded their ship, stole the map to Manila, and a few days later intercepted one of the galleons. Drake informed Queen Elizabeth of his windfall, and from that day on, Acapulco was under constant siege by the likes of British pirates Thomas Cavendish, Henry Morgan, and William Dampier. (Treasure is still said to be buried off La Roqueta Island.) The first fort, the Castillo de San Diego, was built in 1616, and even it could not stave off the Dutch Prince of Nassau, who pillaged the city in 1624. The galleon crews arriving from Manila, exhausted from their journey and suffering from malnutrition (food generally rotted during the long sea voyages), were never a match for the corsairs, well-fed from the excellent fishing in the Gulf of California.

An earthquake destroyed the fort in 1776; its replacement, the Fuerte de San Diego, dates from 1783. In 1799, King Carlos IV declared Acapulco an official city, but shortly thereafter, its decline set in. With the independence movement in 1810, the fair was suspended; the arriving *nao* found the beaches deserted, and the captain was told to take his ship to San Blas. That same year insurgent leader José Maria Morelos attacked Acapulco and a long and bloody siege ensued. The Acapulqueños, who were not particularly enthused by the prospect of losing the source of their livelihood, preferred continued allegiance with the Spanish empire to the dubitable gains of independence. Acapulco, as an important source of revenue for Spain, was a natural target for the rebels, and Morelos burned it in 1814 to destroy its value.

The independence movement and the resulting power struggles brought decades of destruction to Acapulco. (The great German explorer, Alexander von Humboldt, in 1811 found it "savage, dismal and romantic.") The United States sent arms to Morelos at Zihuatanejo, and at one point a truce was declared to enable the outnumbered Royalists to carry corpses from the fortress to a ditch. After Morelos's victory, Acapulco again fell into Royalist hands, and was retaken by Montes de Oca in 1816. In 1820, General Iturbide—later Emperor Agustín I—arrived, seizing the *nao* cargo. In 1831, the insurgent Vicente Guerrero (one-time president of Mexico, for whom the State of Guerrero is named) fled to Acapulco, where he was captured in a famous act of treachery. Picaluga, a Genoese sea captain in the pay of the Royalists, guaranteed Guerrero safe passage on his ship, the *Colombo*. But as soon as Guerrero boarded, he was seized and bound. Picaluga received his $50,000 reward, and Guerrero was executed in Huatulco.

Despite a devastating cholera outbreak in 1850, Acapulco enjoyed a brief revival in the 1850s, a product of the California gold rush. Ships stopped in Acapulco on their way to the Isthmus of Panama, and returned to San Francisco carrying Mexican textiles. (Coincidentally, the great-grandson of

"49er" John Sutter, Ricardo Morlet Sutter, was Acapulco's municipal president in the 1960s.) And in 1855 Benito Juárez, widely considered the father of modern Mexico, was sent to Acapulco to help bring down the dictator Santa Anna. A few years later, the city was bombarded by a French squadron during Juárez's fight against Emperor Maximilian, who had recognized Acapulco's strategic importance.

Acapulco resumed its fitful slumber through most of the 19th and early 20th centuries, although there are some curious anecdotes from that period. In 1875, a young Catholic woman was married to a "Mr. Morris" in the Protestant Chapel of San José. The outraged Catholic population then murdered the groom with a machete, leading to still more bloodshed. In 1892, festivities reminiscent of the days of the Fair of the Americas were held to celebrate the fourth centenary of Columbus's discovery, and a grandiose New Year's Eve ball in 1899 heralded in the new century. An earthquake nearly razed Acapulco in 1909; two years later the city was invaded by some rebellious *lobos*—Afro-Indians from the neighboring Costa Chica region descended from escaped slaves—who threw off the yoke of a tyrant, Johann Schmidt, during the early years of the Mexican Revolution. Otherwise, that bloody era seems to have bypassed Acapulco, probably because, at the time, the city had nothing anyone wanted. Nonetheless, it was the *Partido obrero de Acapulco*—the Acapulco workers' party, supporters of revolutionary leader, and future president, Alvaro Obregón—that first pushed for construction of a road to Mexico City in the 1920s. And in 1920, the Prince of Wales, Edward VIII, anchored in Acapulco for a few brief hours to sample the fishing. As there were no diplomatic relations between Mexico and Great Britain then because of the Mexican Revolution, he had no official reception.

Modern Acapulco dates to the 1920s, when wealthy Mexicans— and adventurous gringos—began frequenting the somnolent village. With the opening of the first highway along Cortés's mule trail in 1928, and initial air service from the capital in 1929, Acapulco began to attract the Hollywood crowd and international statesmen. President Lázaro Cárdenas (1934–40) started public works; the first telephone service began in 1936.

Ironically, it was Cárdenas's nationalism that modernized Mexico's hotel industry, thereby paving the way for the early foreign hotel entrepreneurs who would later dominate that sector of the economy. Cárdenas prohibited foreigners both from owning property within 50 kilometers of the Mexican coastline and from buying hotels. Foreigners circumvented the law either by becoming Mexican citizens or by setting up dummy corporations.

Thus, it was a Texan, Albert B. Pullen, who first formed a company in the 1930s to develop the beautiful Peninsula de las Playas—now known as Old Acapulco—where many of Acapulco's first hotels rose. Pullen became a millionaire in the process. A real estate boom soon followed. J. Paul Getty was alleged to have purchased 900 acres of land at 3 cents an acre, some of which he used to build the Pierre Marqués ("Pierre" after his New York hotel of that name; "Marqués" after Cortés). In 1933, Carlos Barnard erected his first bungalows at El Mirador, atop the cliffs at La Quebrada, and other hotels followed suit.

But despite the growing tourist traffic, Acapulco still had the look, and appeal, of a humble town. Writers flocked there: the reclusive B. Traven, author of *Treasure of the Sierra Madre*, ran a restaurant there from 1929 to 1947. Malcolm Lowry (*Under the Volcano*) first saw Mexico from his Acapulco-bound ship on November 2, 1936; that four-month sojourn was spent sampling the charms of tequila, pulque, mezcal, and Mexican beer. The playwright Sherwood Anderson visited Acapulco in 1938, and Tennessee Williams spent the summer of 1940 there. (Acapulco is, in fact, the setting for *The Night of the Iguana*, his celebrated play that John Huston later filmed in Puerto Vallarta.) That same year, Jane and Paul Bowles, the "bohemian" writer-couple, rented a house there, complete with avocado and lemon trees, a hammock, and their own tropical menagerie. At that time Acapulco boasted dirt roads, a wooden pier, no electricity, and a lot of mosquitoes.

Well-heeled foreigners first became interested in Acapulco during World War II, when most other pleasure spots were off-limits. In 1947, a two-lane highway improved accessibility, cutting travel time from Mexico City to a day and a half. By then there were 28,000 residents, an increase of 25,000 over 1931.

It was President Miguel Alemán Valdes (1946–52) who is credited with turning Acapulco into a tourist destination. Alemán ordered roads paved, streets laid out, water piped in, and public buildings erected. Acapulco received one of its many epithets, "Paradise of America." Even after his presidency, when he directed the newly formed National Tourism Council, Alemán was instrumental in the town's development. He was responsible for the new four-lane super-highway, which in 1955 made it possible to reach Acapulco from Mexico City in just six hours. Alemán himself had a palatial home at Pichilingue Beach, on Puerto Marqués Bay; a personal friend of Conrad Hilton and U.S. ambassador William O'Dwyer, he was one of many Acapulco weekenders to make a fortune out of tourism.

The jet-setters' invasion of Acapulco reached its peak in the 1940s and '50s. While many of them owned homes there, they still liked to congregate at primarily two hotels. Las Brisas was built in 1954 as a small cottage colony, Bermuda-style, by Juan March, on the former site of the fortress. The other watering hole was the Villa Vera Racquet Club. Originally a private residence for an Omaha businessman, it was later managed by Ernest Henri ("Teddy") Stauffer, a Swiss swing bandleader who had fled the Nazis and settled in Acapulco, where he became affectionately known as "Mr. Acapulco." Stauffer also put up Acapulco's first discotheque, Tequila A Go-Go, and took over the popular La Perla restaurant at La Quebrada, home to the cliff divers. The Villa Vera boasted one of Acapulco's many innovations, the first swim-up bar, and its first tennis club. (Another Acapulco first was parasailing.)

Lana Turner used to frequent the Villa Vera's piano bar. Elizabeth Taylor married Mike Todd there, with Debbie Reynolds and Eddie Fisher as witnesses. JFK honeymooned in Acapulco, as did Brigitte Bardot and, many years later, Henry Kissinger. Yugoslav President Tito stayed there for 38 days, in one of 76 private homes owned by Las Brisas. President Eisenhower's visit in 1959 brought Acapulco even more publicity, as did an international film festival that debuted that year. Acapulco's guest list filled the society pages and gossip columns of America and Europe: Frank Sinatra, Johnny Weissmuller, New York Mayor Robert Wagner, Harry Belafonte, Douglas Fairbanks, Jr., Judy Garland, Sir Anthony Eden, John Wayne, Gina Lollobrigida, Gary Cooper, Edgar Bronfman, Jimmy Stewart, the Guinness family, Richard Widmark, Baron de Rothschild. . . .

By the late 1950s and early '60s Acapulco, which had also acquired the sobriquet "Nirvana by the Sea," was being called "Miami on the Pacific." It had long since ceased to be the exclusive haven for the rich and famous: Hotel construction had mushroomed, and the city's infrastructure could not keep pace with the growing resident population, then 100,000. La Laja, a seedy cluster of tenements outside town lacking sewers, drinking water, and electricity, swelled with 8,000 minimum-wage hotel workers known as *paracaidistas* (parachutists), or squatters. The government tried discreetly to squelch the city's social problems by selling the land at La Laja to the squatters, but also feared that move would encourage even more migration and aggravate unemployment. Hundreds of locals—mostly Indians from the surrounding region—were reduced to roaming the beaches, peddling kitschy folk art, tie-dyed beachwear, suntan oil, and soda.

By the mid-1960s, the government was eyeing the Port of Acapulco with renewed interest as a way to balance the economy and offset the seasonality of tourism. Acapulco was again trading, primarily with the Orient, and in 1963 some 180 freighters arrived, laden with Japanese appliances and automobiles. Each year, 60,000 tons of copra—dried coconut meat, used for making soap and margarine—left port; the copra industry was second to tourism in the region. The government wanted to capitalize on Acapulco's revived trade status by building a new port and opening a railroad to convey all the imports and locally produced copra, rubber, and wood pulp to Mexico City. But the projects never got off the ground.

So tourism—which generated $50 million a year in direct spending—remained the key to Acapulco. With the advent of international jet travel in 1964, and the start-up of nonstop service from the United States in 1966, Acapulco's ascendancy became even more spectacular. The once lowly airport was dressed up in marble, and countless foreigners arrived to set up fashion boutiques and restaurants and indulge in the lucrative trade of marijuana and cocaine. Media stories continued to appear with great regularity, focusing largely on Merle Oberon Pagliai, the queen of Acapulco society who spent six months a year in Acapulco in her Moorish-style villa, El Ghalal. Needless to say, that abode was as lavish as the nightly parties thrown about town by her fellow travelers, where socks were prohibited and themed events varied from disco nights (accompanied by the sounds of the Beach Boys) to costume frolics (all invitees dressed as Charles Addams characters). *Coco locos*—a mouthful of coconut juice with a generous serving of rum, gin, or tequila, inevitably presented in a coconut shell—were all the rage.

But Acapulco's clients in the '60s—and today still—were not only the Beautiful People, who considered it simply another stop on their yearly perambulations, with good weather, air-conditioning, and more isolation from the "commoners" than could be found in Jamaica or Miami. (Though officially all the beaches are publicly owned, the wealthy have always found ways to enjoy themselves in private.) The majority were actually Mexicans, to whom Acapulco was the equivalent of Atlantic City. Additionally, there were vacationing college students—frequently indulging in midnight surf-dancing—seamen, and middle-class Americans who felt comfortable with the American-brand fast-food outlets lining the Costera Alemán, a south-of-the-border Coney Island.

Commercialization and unbridled growth took their toll on Acapulco in the 1970s. Belatedly, the government planned a $14 million project to pipe the city's sewage out to sea; prior to that the sewage had simply been carried in an open canal, and the hotels had installed their own services. Having reached the mature stage of its development, Acapulco found its glamour and popularity waning. That may have been a godsend for its 300,000 residents, crowded to the breaking point, as rural unrest in the surrounding countryside led increasingly to outbursts of violence. In the early 1970s, guerrillas assassinated Acapulco's police chief, kidnapped the state senator, and occasionally took hostages in Acapulco itself before most of the group was killed in gun battles. (As recently as 1980, tourists traveling by bus to the State of Guerrero have been stopped by soldiers on the lookout for illegal weapons.)

Acapulco, Mexico's phenomenally successful showpiece and a classic model worldwide for tourism development, served as the basis for what to do and what not to do in subsequent Mexican resorts. As Acapulco waned, Mexico began looking elsewhere to practice its magic. In Ixtapa, Cancún, Los Cabos, and now Huatulco, the government is attempting to avoid the mistakes it made in Acapulco through careful planning, while duplicating its formula of sea, sand, and sex. Several of those destinations now siphon off the tourism business. Whereas in the 1960s, foreigners represented 45 percent of Acapulco's tourist revenue, by the mid-1980s that figure had slipped to 32 percent. It was not just that foreigners preferred Cancún, where they could be truly isolated from the natives; it was that Cancún was priced way beyond the reach of the average Mexican.

But Acapulqueños, who for centuries have derived their livelihood from commerce with foreigners, are intent on keeping their city afloat. In 1988, a consortium of government agencies banded together to refurbish the area known as Traditional Acapulco, centered around Caleta Beach and the Zócalo. Hotels are being spruced up, street vendors are being paid to relocate to public markets, and the streets are undergoing a face-lift. And although one-third of Acapulco's one million residents still live in slums, that fact seldom intrudes on the tourist's conscience. In terms of sheer size, Acapulco is still the biggest of Mexico's tourist destinations. To many, it continues to epitomize the glamour and vitality for which it has long been celebrated. And though it will go through more permutations, Acapulco holds a secure place in Mexico's future.

The Cliff Dive

by Craig Vetter

Chicago is home for freelance writer Craig Vetter.

Just before the divers at La Quebrada in Acapulco take the long fall from the cliff into the surf, they kneel at a little shrine to Our Lady of Guadalupe and say their prayers. It's not hard to imagine what they ask her—I used to know the prayers they know—probably something like, "Remember, O most gracious Virgin, that never was it known that anyone who fled to thy intercession or sought thy mercy was left unaided. Inspired by this confidence, I fly to thee, O Virgin of Virgins, my Mother. To thee I come, before thee I stand, sinful and sorrowful. O Mother of the word incarnate, despise not my petitions but in thy mercy hear and answer me: Let the water be deep enough, let the current be gentle, save me from garbage on the water, from the rocks, from blindness, from death, and may the *turistas* drop at least ten pesos apiece into the hat before they haul their fat white bodies back onto the buses."

I watched them dive half a dozen times one day. I sat on the terrace of the Mirador Hotel that overlooks the cliff with tequila and beer in front of me, telling myself I was trying to decide whether or not I would do this thing. I knew that the power of prayer wouldn't get me into the air off that rock. I've dived from heights before, but never that high, never out over rocks like those, never into a slash of water as narrow as that. Still, the only reason I was down there in the good tropical sun was to dive or to come up with an eloquent string of reasons why I hadn't. As it was, every time a Mexican dived, I was adding a because to my list of why nots.

One of them would walk out onto the rock and look down at the surf 130 feet below him. Then he'd kneel at the shrine, cross himself and pray. When he got up, he'd wander out of sight for a moment behind the little statue of Mary, then come back and stand for another five minutes on the edge while the tourists crowded the railings of the hotel terrace and filled the vantage points on the rocks below. Then he'd put both arms out straight in front of him, drop them to his sides, cock his legs, roll forward, and then spring with what looked like all his strength into a perfect flying arch. Foam boils up where the divers go in and the sound when they hit the water is like an old cannon going off. Then, a few seconds later, he'd be up, waving one arm and treading water against the white surge that was trying to slap him up onto the rocks.

After a couple of divers and a couple of tequilas, I was telling myself I could live through it. I'd probably get hurt real bad, but it wouldn't kill me. I could get out past those rocks, all right, then it would just be a matter of going into the water as straight and skinny and strong as I could. I figured the worst I could get would be a broken back. Or else . . . or else I could sit right there on that terrace, have another shot of Cuervo, maybe six, lay back on my laurels and review the risks already taken. The worst I could get would be a hangover.

One of the divers came around to collect 50 cents. I gave him a dollar and when he said that was too much, I told him no, it wasn't. His name was Fidel and he had a broad face and a paunch that hung out over his tight red trunks. He looked about 40 years old. I asked him what kind of injuries the *clavadistas* got when they didn't hit the water right. Broken bones, he told me, when the arms sometimes collapse into the head on impact. And the eyes, he said, if you break the water eyes first instead of with the top of your head, you go blind. But they have an association, he said, and the 26 divers in it have a fund, so that if one of them is hurt or killed, his family is taken care of. I didn't ask him if there was a fund for half-wit gringos with a history of foolish moments and a little too much sauce in them. There are no funds for people like that, people like me. Just simple services when the time comes.

Fidel moved off through the crowd, looking for more peso notes, and pretty much left me thinking there was no way in hell I was going to make that dive. The idea that I'd probably survive the plunge didn't mean nearly as much after he told me about the arms snapping over the head on entry. Somehow, I could *hear* that one. Even from 40 or 45 feet, which is the highest I've ever dived, you hit the water hard enough to make a moron out of yourself if you do it wrong. It *hurts* even when you do it right.

Finally, that afternoon, I figured out exactly what that cliff was to me. It wasn't a test of guts, or coordination, or strength, or Zen oneness with this imaginary existence. It was an intelligence test, the most fundamental kind of intelligence test: If you're intelligent, you don't *take* the test. Still, to sit there and think it through was one thing. I knew I had to let the animal make the final decision; take the meat up there onto that rock and let it look down the throat of this thing, let it *feel* the edge. There'd be no more maybes after that.

You actually have to climb down the rocks from the hotel to the spot from which they dive. On my way, I kept waiting for someone to stop me, tell me it was divers only out there, but no one did and there were no warning signs. I jumped a low stone wall and crept down some rock steps overhung with trees that made it feel like a tunnel out the end of which I could see the backside of the little shrine. It was cement, painted silver, and behind it, stacked like cordwood—as if to say that even among religious people liquor takes up where prayer leaves off—were two dozen empty tequila bottles. Two steps beyond that and I was out from under the green overhead and on the small flat pad from which they do it, and the scene opened before me: to my left, the hotel. I could see people tapping each other and pointing at me, as if to say, "Here goes another one, Edith." To my right, the flat blue Pacific stretched out to a sharp tropical horizon, and then turned into sky. I stepped up and hung my toes over the edge, and then looked down at the rocks below me, then at the rocks on the other side, then at the skinny finger of water between them, rising and falling, foaming in and out. There were Styrofoam cups on the tide, pieces of cardboard and other trash I couldn't make out. I remembered my mother, who was a champion swimmer in the '30s, telling me about a woman high diver who'd gone off a 100-foot tower in Atlantic City and hit an orange peel on the water. She lived, but the image of their hauling her limp from the water has stayed with me, and it was never more vivid than at that moment at La Quebrada. Looking down from that cliff, your perspective is so hopelessly distorted it seems that, to miss the rocks on your side of the channel, you'd have to throw yourself onto the rocks on the other side. I tried to imagine myself through it. Get steady, feet together, arms down, roll, push, arch . . . but I couldn't take the fantasy any further than that. "No," I said out loud. "Just turn around and say goodbye to the Lady, Craig."

A couple of hours later, the defeat of the thing didn't seem very profound at all. If I'd kept drinking tequila, I just might have gone screaming off that cliff. Tequila, after all, talks to the animal in you and *he* thinks he can do anything when he's drunk.

After all, you gotta stop somewhere.

3 Essential Information

Arriving and Departing

By Train There is no train service from the United States or Canada to Mexico.

By Bus Two bus lines operate frequent service from Mexico City. The trip takes about 6 hours. Most buses are comfortable and air-conditioned. *Tasqueña* has deluxe service to the terminal in Old Acapulco at Cuauhtemoc and Magallanes streets (tel. 748/5–95–60). *Flecha Roja's* second-class coaches come to the station at Cuauhtemoc 97 (tel. 748/2–03–51).

By Car Though we don't recommend driving to Acapulco from the United States or Canada, the main entry roads are Route 200 from the north and Route 95 from Mexico City.

From Center City to the Airport The best, and easiest, way to reach the airport is by hotel taxi. The 20- to 25-minute ride is $15–$20.

Important Addresses and Numbers

Tourist Information The State of Guerrero Department of Tourism (SEFOTUR) will help you find your way around and answer questions. The office is in the Centro Internacional, tel. 748/4–70–50. It is open Mon. through Sat. from 9 to 2 and from 5 to 7 PM. The Secretaría de Tourismo, across from the Super-Super, Costera Miguel Alemán 187, is open 8–3:30 weekdays, 10–2 Sat. Closed Sun. The staff speaks English, has brochures and maps on other parts of Mexico, and can help you find a hotel room. Tel. 748/5–10–41 or 5–13–04.

Embassies The consular representative for the United States is Bonny Urbaneck. Her office is in the Club del Sol Hotel on the Costera, tel. 5–72–07. The Canadian representative is Diane McLean de Huerta, and her office is on the mezzanine level of the Club del Sol Hotel, tel. 5–66–21.

Emergencies **Police,** tel. 3–36–28 or 3–28–32.

The **Red Cross** can be reached at tel. 5–41–00 or 5–41–01. Two hospitals that treat foreigners are **Hospital Privado Magallanes,** Wilfrido Massiu 2, tel. 5–65–44; and **Hospital Centro Médico,** J. Arevalo 99, tel. 2–46–92. Your hotel, the Secretaría de Turismo and Servicios Médicos Turísticos (SEME), tel. 4–32–60, can locate an English-speaking doctor. But they don't come cheap—house calls are about $50. The Secretaría de Turismo has a list of dentists and suggests Dr. Guadalupe Carmona, Costera Miguel Alemán 220–101, tel. 5–71–76; or Dr. Juvenal Uriostegui, Clínica Médica Sor Juana, Ruiz Cortínez 1, tel. 7–11–51.

English Bookstores English-language books and periodicals can be found at Sanborns, a reputable American-style department store chain, and at the newsstands in some of the larger hotels. Most reading material costs more than at home. Many small newsstands and the Super-Super carry the *Mexico City News,* an English-language daily newspaper with a large Sunday edition carrying reports from many cities including Acapulco. Social events and evening activities in Acapulco are often covered. Every day several pages are devoted to foreign news drawn from the wire services with reprints of articles from the *Washington Post, New York Times,* and *Los Angeles Times. Time* and *Newsweek* magazines are also available.

Travel Agencies *American Express* is at Costera Miguel Alemán 709, tel. 4–60–60. *Thomas Cook's* representative in Acapulco is *Viajes Wagon-Lits,* at Costera Miguel Alemán 239 (Las Hamacas Hotel), tel. 2–28–61; and Scenic Highway 5255 (Las Brisas Hotel), tel. 4–09–91.

Staying in Touch

Telephone Due to constant development in Acapulco and other parts of Mexico, phone numbers are constantly being added and changed. This is a fact of life in Mexico.

Local Calls A working pay phone is as rare as a cloudy day in Acapulco. If you find one that works, use it immediately. You may never see one again. Seriously, pay phones are in short supply, though you can find some in the Zócalo and along the Costera Miguel Alemán. Just look for the lines of bored Mexicans, and prepare for a wait of up to 15 minutes. Operators take a long time to answer, especially in the afternoon and on weekends. You may have to make several attempts. Pay phone is a misnomer; all public phones in Mexico have been free since the earthquake in 1985.

International Calls At your hotel, the operator can put calls through. Surcharges vary, but a good rule of thumb is that the more expensive the hotel, the more expensive the call. In a four-star hotel the surcharge will be about $4, which applies even if you are calling collect. Long-distance charges are exorbitant. To call the United States costs about $4 a minute; to call Europe costs about $12 a minute. The cheapest way to phone is collect. Just go to a phone booth and dial 09. English-speaking operators take a while to answer, but they put calls through immediately. There are also *casetas,* little phone stores that put through long-distance calls within Mexico and overseas. There is no surcharge at *casetas,* but they don't handle collect calls. There are several near the Zócalo and on the Costera. Most close for siesta but stay open until 8 PM.

Mail The main post office is on the Costera in Old Acapulco, one
Postal Rates block west of Sanborns. Weekdays it is open 8 AM–8 PM, weekends 9 AM–1 PM. You can also send telegrams from this post office. A letter to the United States takes about 10 days, about two weeks to Europe. Rates for postcards and letters are the same: Up to 10 grams to Canada runs about 40¢, about 50¢ to Europe. You can buy postcards and envelopes in all sizes from vendors outside the post office. If the postcards you are mailing are small, put them in an envelope, or the stamps will cover the address. We don't recommend you mail anything other than a postcard or letter from Mexico. It may never reach its destination.

Receiving Mail If you aren't sure where you will be staying, you can receive mail at the general post office (Lista de Correos, Officina Central, Costera Miguel Alemán 215, Acapulco 39301, Gro. Mexico). If you have an American Express card or traveler's checks, you can receive mail at the American Express office, (Costera Miguel Alemán 709, Acapulco, Gro., Mexico).

If officials can't find your letter, ask them to look under your first name or middle initial because Mexicans often have two last names and so have a different system for filing letters.

Getting Around

Getting around in Acapulco is quite simple. You can walk to many places and the bus costs only 20¢. Taxis cost less than in the United States, so most tourists quickly become avid taxi takers.

By Bus The buses tourists use the most are those that go from Puerto Marqués to Caleta and stop at the fairly conspicuous metal bus stops along the way. If you want to go from the Zócalo to The Strip, catch the bus that says "La Base" (the naval base near the Exelaris Hyatt Regency). This bus detours through Old Acapulco and returns to the Costera just east of the Ritz Hotel. If you want to follow the Costera for the entire route take the bus marked "Hornos." The price is about 20¢. Buses to Pie de la Cuesta or Puerto Marqués say so on the front. The Puerto Marqués bus runs about every half hour and is always crowded.

By Taxi We could write an entire guide on taxis in Acapulco as there are so many different kinds with varying prices. The first thing to understand is that you will never pay as little as the Mexicans —the most expensive fare for non-gringos is $1.50. That is another fact of life in Mexico. On the bright side, taxis are still cheaper than at home. How much you pay depends on what type of taxi you get.

The most expensive are hotel taxis. A price list that all drivers adhere to is posted in hotel lobbies. Fares in town are usually about $4; a ride to the Princess Hotel or Caleta beach is about $7. Hotel taxis are by far the plushest and kept in the best condition.

Cabs that cruise with their roof light off occasionally carry a price list. But don't expect to find a running meter, as they are all mysteriously "broken." You need to reach an agreement with these drivers, but the fare should be less than at a hotel. There is a minimum charge of 50¢. Some taxis that cruise have hotel or restaurant names stenciled on the side, but are not affiliated with any establishment. Before you go anywhere by cab, find out what the price should be and agree with the driver on a price. You can usually convince one to overcharge you by only 50¢ or $1. Alternatively, you can hand them the correct fare when you arrive, but that can lead to a nasty scene where the driver is disappointed to receive the correct fare and argues with you for more.

The cheapest taxis are the little Volkswagens. Officially there is a 50¢ minimum charge, but the Mexicans don't stick to it. A normal, i.e., Mexican-priced fare, is $1 to go from the Zócalo to American Express, but lots of luck getting a taxi driver to accept that from a tourist. Rates are about 50¢ higher at night and, though tipping is not expected, Mexicans usually leave small change.

You can also hire a taxi by the hour or the day, which means that you can have one take you to Pie de la Cuesta or wait while you do your shopping. Prices vary from about $12 an hour for a hotel taxi to $8 an hour for a street taxi. Never let a taxi driver decide where you should eat or shop since many get kickbacks from some of the smaller stores and restaurants. In fact if you look carefully, you can see people waiting outside of various destinations; their job is to note down the cab's license plate numbers and pay them when they return later for a 10% commission.

By Motorscooter Little Honda motorscooters can be rented from a stand outside CiCi, the children's water park on the Costera. They are also available at the Plaza Hotel. Cost: $8 an hour or $30 per day.

By Horse and Carriage Buggy rides up and down The Strip are available on weekends. Bargain before you get in—prices are about $20 for half an hour.

Tipping

Restaurants: 15%

Waiters in discos: 15%

Porters: $1 per suitcase

Doormen in luxury hotel: 50¢ for carrying suitcases to front desk

Doormen in moderate hotel: Optional, but usually 50¢ for carrying bags to front desk

Bellhops in moderate or luxury hotel: $1 per suitcase

Guided Tours

There are organized tours everywhere in Acapulco, from the red-light district to the lagoon. Tours to Mexican fiestas in the evenings or the markets in the daytime are easy to arrange. Tour operators have offices around town and desks in many of the large hotels. If your hotel can't arrange a tour, contact *Consejeros de Viajes* at the Torre de Acapulco, Costera Miguel Alemán 1252, tel. 4–74–00; *Acuario*, Costera Miguel Alemán, opposite the Plaza Hotel, tel. 5–61–00; or *see* Excursions.

4 Exploring Acapulco

Orientation

Acapulco is a city that is easily understood, easily explored. During the day the focus for most visitors is the beach and the myriad of activities that happen on and off it—sunbathing, swimming, waterskiing, parasailing, snorkeling, deep-sea fishing, and so on. At night, the attention shifts to the restaurants and discos. The Costera Miguel Alemán, the wide boulevard that hugs Acapulco Bay from the Scenic Highway to Caleta Beach (a distance of nearly eight miles), is central to both day and night diversions. All the major beaches, big hotels—minus the more-exclusive East Bay properties, such as Las Brisas, Pierre Marqués, and the Princess—and shopping malls are off the Costera. Hence most of the shopping, dining, and clubbing takes place within a few blocks of the Costera, and many an address is listed only as "Costera Miguel Alemán." Because street addresses are not often used and streets have no logical pattern, directions are usually given from a major landmark, such as CiCi or the Zócalo.

Old Acapulco, the colonial part of town, is where the Mexicans go to run their errands: mail letters at the post office, buy supplies at the Mercado Municipal, and have clothes made/repaired at the tailor. Here is where you'll find the Zócalo, the church, and Fort San Diego. Just up the hill from Old Acapulco is La Quebrada, where, five times a day, the cliff divers plunge into the surf 130 feet below.

The peninsula just south of Old Acapulco contains remnants of the first version of Acapulco. This primarily residential area was prey to dilapidation and abandonment of late but is being revitalized, with the reopening of the Caleta Hotel on Caleta Beach as its first phase. The Plaza de Toros (bullfights are Sundays at 5 PM from December through Easter) is in the center of the peninsula.

If you've arrived by plane, you've had a royal introduction to Acapulco Bay. Driving from the airport, via the Scenic Highway, the first thing you see on your left is the golf course for the Acapulco Princess. Just over the hill is your first glimpse of the entire bay, and it is truly gorgeous, day or night. Your tour continues after you've settled into your hotel.

Lovers of art and architecture and devotees of historic monuments should not expect a wealth of sites, and that's as it should be. Acapulco is perfect for those who enjoy relaxing at the beach and pool by day and gearing up for dining and dancing at night. And though there are sights worth seeing outside of Old Acapulco that can be reached easily on foot, that route is not recommended. Walking along the Costera with its traffic and congestion can be rather unpleasant, especially in the heat. If you do fancy an ambulatory tour, we suggest a stroll along the beach, stopping en route at one of the hotel bars for an ice-cold daiquiri or frosty *cerveza* (beer).

Taxis are another inexpensive option. They cost about the equivalent of a bus ride in the United States (*see* Getting Around in Essential Information About Acapulco for details on the best places to hire a cab). Buses are dirt-cheap, but slow and not air-conditioned. There are also tour operators eager to show you around. Consult the list of tour operators (*see* Guided Tours in Essential Information About Acapulco), or check the activities desk at the major hotels. A tour is also handy if you don't have a car and want to explore the lagoons east and west of Acapulco (*see* Excursions).

The numbers in the margins correspond with the numbered points of interest on the map on page 44 – 45.

① **La Base,** the Mexican naval base next to Plaza Icacos, anchors the eastern terminus of the Costera. There are no tours.

② The **Centro Cultural de Acapulco** is on the beach side of the Costera, just past the Exelaris Hyatt Regency hotel. It contains a small archaeological museum and the Zochipala art gallery with changing exhibits. *Open weekdays, 9–1 and 5–8. Free.*

③ CiCi (short for Centro Internacional para Convivencia Infantil) on the Costera, is a water-oriented theme park for children. There are dolphin and seal shows, a freshwater pool with wave-making apparatus, water slide, mini-aquarium and other attractions. *Open daily 10–6. Admission: $3 adults; $2 children, extra charge for water slide.*

④ A bit past CiCi, on the right side of the Costera, is **Centro Internacional** (the Convention Center), not really of interest unless you plan to do some shopping in one of the handfuls of stores within or are attending a conference there. *Open weekdays 9–5.*

⑤ Continue along the Costera, through the heart of The Strip, until you reach **Papagayo Park,** one of the top municipal parks in the country for location, beauty, and variety. Named for the hotel that formerly occupied the grounds, Papagayo sits on 52 acres of prime real estate on the Costera, just after the underpass at the end of The Strip. Though aimed at children, there is plenty for all ages to enjoy. Youngsters enjoy the life-size model of a Spanish galleon like the ones that once sailed into Acapulco while it was Mexico's capital for trade with the Orient. There is a racetrack with mite-size Can Am cars; a replica of the space shuttle *Columbia;* bumper boats in a lagoon, and other rides. The Aviary is Papagayo's best feature: Hundreds of species of birds flitter overhead as you amble down shaded paths. *Open weekdays 2:30–9:30 PM, weekends 3:30–11:30 PM. Admission free, though rides cost 25¢–50¢. Rides closed Tues.*

⑥ The sprawling **Mercado Municipal,** a few blocks from the Costera, is Acapulco at its most authentic. It is also the city's answer to the suburban shopping mall. Locals come to purchase their everyday needs, from fresh vegetables and candles to plastic buckets and love potions. (Many cab drivers get a 10% commission on whatever you buy at the nearby Artesanías Finas de Acapulco (AFA), so many will try to discourage you from going to the mercado. Their reasons are highly imaginative, such as "The mercado's souvenirs are covered with dangerous lead-based paint." Just ignore them.) Go between 10 AM and 1 PM and ask to be dropped off near the *flores* (flower stand) closest to the souvenir and craft section. If you've driven to the mercado, locals may volunteer to watch your car; be sure to lock your trunk and tip at least 50¢.

The stalls within the mercado are densely packed together but luckily are awning-covered, so things stay quite cool despite

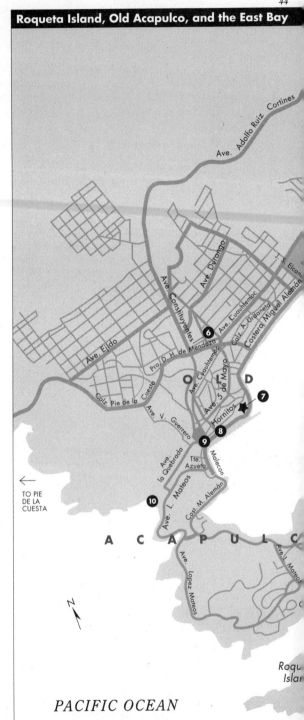

44

Roqueta Island, Old Acapulco, and the East Bay

PACIFIC OCEAN

TO PIE
DE LA
CUESTA

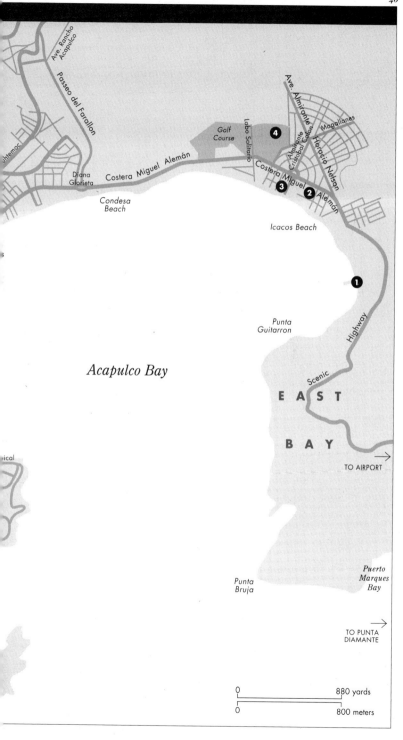

Ave. Rancho Acapulco

Passeo del Farallon

Cuhtemoc

Diana Glorieta

Costera Miguel Alemán

Condesa Beach

Golf Course

Lobo Solitario

Ave. Almirante Cristobal Colón

Ave. Almirante Horacio Nelson

Magallanes

4

Costera Miguel Alemán

3

2

Icacos Beach

1

Punta Guitarron

Acapulco Bay

Highway

Scenic

E A S T

B A Y

TO AIRPORT →

ical

Punta Bruja

Puerto Marques Bay

TO PUNTA DIAMANTE →

| 0 | 880 yards |
| 0 | 800 meters |

the lack of air-conditioning. From the flower stall, as you face the ceramic stand, turn right and head into the market. There are hundreds of souvenirs to choose from: woven blankets, puppets, colorful wooden toys and plates, leather goods, baskets, hammocks, and handmade wooden furniture including child-size chairs. You can also find some kitschy gems: Acapulco ashtrays and boxes covered with tiny shells, or enormous framed pictures of the Virgin of Guadalupe. Bargaining hard is the rule: Start at half the asking price. The exception is silver. Under no circumstance pay more than one-fourth the asking price for hallmarked jewelry. A bracelet will be offered for $50 but the price should drop to less than $20 within five minutes. The silver vendors speak English.

The mercado is patronized primarily by Mexicans and, like many markets, is divided into departments. One area sells locally made brushes and wooden spoons. In another, artisans put finishing touches on baskets and wooden furniture. Women sells rows of neatly arranged plastic buckets in a rainbow of colors. There are dozens of exotic blossoms—many arranged into FTD-like centerpieces—in the flower market. Prices are a fraction of what you'd pay at home. The beans, spices, and vegetable section has a number of unfamiliar tropical products. There is even a stand offering medicinal herbs from China along with good luck charms. The love potions have unusual packaging. "Take one home to dominate your mate or to effect a reconciliation" the label on one says. Allow at least an hour and a half to take it all in.

7 Built in the 18th century to protect the city from pirates, **El Fuerte de San Diego** is up on the hill overlooking the harbor next to the army barracks in Old Acapulco. (The original fort, destroyed in an earthquake, was built in 1616.) The fort now houses the **Museo Historico de Acapulco,** under the auspices of Mexico City's prestigious Museum of Anthropology. The exhibits portray the city from prehistoric times through Mexico's independence from Spain in 1821. Especially noteworthy are the displays touching on the Christian missionaries sent from Mexico to the Far East and the cultural interchange that resulted. Exhibits are mounted in separate air-conditioned rooms of the old fort. In addition to the permanent collection, there are changing exhibits and a projection room. The museum sponsors lectures (in Spanish), meetings, and an occasional evening performance. The front desk has details. *Open Tues.– Sat. 10–6, Sun. 10–5. Closed Mon. Admission: 30¢. Tel. 748/3–97–30.*

8 Acapulco is still a lively commercial port and fishing center. If you stroll along the **waterfront,** you'll see all these activities at the commercial docks. The cruise ships dock here, and at night Mexican parents bring their children to play in the small tree-lined promenade. Further west, by the Zócalo, are the docks for the sightseeing yachts and smaller fishing boats. It's a good spot to join the Mexicans in people-watching.

9 The **Zócalo** is the center of Old Acapulco, a shaded plaza in front of **Nuestra Señora de la Soledad,** the town's modern but unusual —stark white exterior with bulb-shaped blue and yellow spires —church. If there is any place in Acapulco that can be called picturesque or authentic, the Zócalo is it. Overgrown with dense trees, it is the hub of downtown, a spot for socializing. All day it is filled with vendors, shoeshine men, and people lining up to use the pay phones. After siesta, they drift here to meet and greet. On Sunday there's music in the grandstand. There are several cafés and news agents selling the English-language *Mexico City News*, so tourists lodging in the area linger here, too. The Flor de Acapulco is a lovely old-fashioned café with a 1950s ambience. Groups of Mexicans stop in for breakfast before work, and in the evening it is popular for drinks and meals. European hippie types and retired Canadians hang out at Flor de Acapulco for hours. Around the Zócalo are several souvenir shops, and on the side streets you can get hefty, fruity milk shakes for about 50¢. The "flea market," inexpensive tailor shops, and Woolworth's (*see* Shopping) are nearby.

Time Out   The café across from the Flor de Acapulco, below the German restaurant, serves *churros* every afternoon beginning at 4. This Spanish treat of fried dough dusted with sugar and dipped in hot chocolate is popular at *merienda*, which means snack.

10   A 10-minute walk up the hill from the Zócalo brings you to **La Quebrada.** This is home to the famous Mirador Hotel and a large silver shop Taxco El Viejo (*see* Shopping). In the 1940s this was the center of action for tourists and it retains an atmosphere reminiscent of its glory days. Most visitors eventually make the trip here because this is where the famous cliff divers jump from a height of 130 feet daily at 1, 7:15, 8:15, 9:15 and 10:30. The sunset and evening dives are especially thrilling. Before they dive, the brave divers say a pray at a small shrine near the jumping-off point. Sometimes they dive in pairs, often they carry torches.

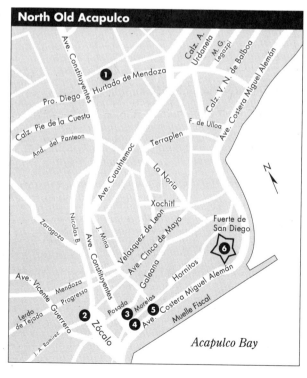

North Old Acapulco

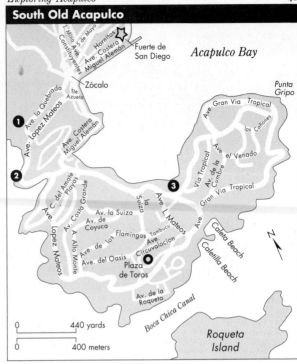

South Old Acapulco

What to See and Do with Children

Palao's. This restaurant on Roqueta Island has a sandy cove for swimming, a pony, and a cage of monkeys that entertain the youngsters. Children enjoy the motorboat ride out to the island (*see* Excursions).

Beto's. Another restaurant catering to children, this is right on the beach at Barra Vieja, with a child-size pool for swimming and a play tower for climbing.

Mimi's Chili Saloon and **Carlos 'n Charlies.** If your child misses familiar food (hamburgers, fries, etc.), these fun eateries will fill the bill as well as young stomachs. The decor of both is colorful and festive.

Waterskiing show at the Colonial Restaurant. Staged near the Fuerte de San Diego, this is a family favorite.

Beaches

The lure of sun and sand is legend in Acapulco. Once you hit the beach, you may never want to leave, and you may never need to except to enjoy Acapulco's other draw, its nightlife. Every sport is available and you can shop from roving souvenir vendors, eat in a beach restaurant, dance, and sleep in a *hamaca* (hammock) without leaving the water's edge. If you want to avoid the crowds, there are also plenty of quiet and even isolated beaches within reach. however, at some of these, such as Revolcadero and Pie de la Cuesta, there is a very strong undertow and strong surf, so swimming is not advised.

Though water sports are available on most beaches, consider the following before you enter the water: Despite an enticing appearance and claims that officials are cleaning up the bay, it remains polluted. If this bothers you, we suggest you follow the lead of the Mexican cognoscenti and take the waters at your hotel pool.

Beaches in Mexico are public, even those that seem to belong to a big hotel. The list below moves from east to west.

Revolcadero   A wide, sprawling beach next to the Pierre Marqués and Princess hotels, its water is shallow and waves fairly rough. People come here to surf and ride horses.

Puerto Marqués   Tucked below the airport highway, this strand is popular with Mexican tourists, so it tends to get crowded on weekends.

Icacos   Stretching from the naval base to Club El Presidente, this beach is less populated than others on The Strip. The morning waves are especially calm.

Condesa   Smack in the middle of Acapulco Bay, this stretch of sand has more than its share of tourists, especially singles. The beachside restaurants are convenient for bites between parasailing flights.

Hornos and Hornitos   Running from the Paraiso Radisson to Las Hamacas hotels, these beaches are shoulder to shoulder with Mexican tourists. They know a good thing: Graceful palms shade the sand and there are scads of casual eateries within walking distance.

Caleta and Caletilla   On the peninsula in Old Acapulco, these two once rivaled La Quebrada as the main tourist area in Acapulco's heyday. Now they attract families. Motorboats to Roqueta leave from this area.

Roqueta Island   A round-trip ferry costs about $1.50 and takes 10 minutes. Mexicans consider Roqueta Island their day-trip spot *(see* Excursions for details).

Pie de la Cuesta   You'll need a car or cab to reach this relatively unpopulated spot about 15 minutes outside of town. A few rustic restaurants border the wide beach and palapas provide *sombra* (shade). (*See* Excursions for details.)

5 Shopping

There is quite a lot of shopping to do in Acapulco, and the abundance of air-conditioned shopping malls and boutiques makes picking up gifts and souvenirs all the more pleasurable. Except for the markets, most places shut for siesta. The typical hours of business are 10–1 and then 4–7, though these hours vary slightly. Most shops close on Sunday.

Though the fall of the peso gives most travelers to Acapulco a shopping edge, those who master the art of bargaining and understand how the Mexican sales tax (IVA) works, will have their purchasing power increased even more.

Bargaining This is essential when dealing with street vendors, in small crafts shops, and in the mercado. Start at just below half the asking price and pay up to two-thirds. Vendors will usually drop the price by about one-third immediately. Then the tooth-pulling stage begins, when you haggle over one or two dollars. The best way to break a deadlock is to walk away and feign disinterest. They will soon come after you with a more reasonable offer.

IVA The standard sales tax in Mexico is known as an IVA, which is short for *impuesto valor añadido* (value tax added). It is 15%. Most purchases, including food, drink, and clothing, are taxed. But don't pay the IVA twice; it is often incorporated into the cost of an item. Look for signs in shop windows alongside the price that say *IVA Incluido*, or ask the shopkeeper if IVA is part of the listed price.

Gift Ideas

Mexicans produce quantities of inexpensive collectibles and souvenirs such as colorful serapes, ceramics, glassware, silver, straw hats, leather, sculptures made of shells, wooden toys, carved walking canes, and, in season, Christmas ornaments. Most of these trinkets can be found everywhere. In fact, you may tire of the hawkers who traverse the beaches and approach passersby on the street. Crafts sold on the street include stone wind chimes, painted wooden birds, (each about $3), earrings made of shells for 25¢, shell sculptures, sets of wooden dishes and rugs. Bargaining is essential in these situations (see Bargaining). Prices are often lower in the markets and on the street, so it makes sense to buy outside of the shops, or visit the shops first, note the prices, and then venture to the markets to try and beat the store prices. Don't buy any article described as "silver" on the street. Street vendors sell a silver facsimile called alpaca. In the mornings they buy bracelets from a wholesale supplier for 50¢ that they sell to unsuspecting tourists in the afternoon for $5. Buy silver in shops and look for the 9.25 hallmark, which means you are getting sterling. The large AFA (Artesanías Finas de Acapulco) crafts shop, though, has fixed prices and will ship, so this is the place to purchase onyx lamp stands and other larger items (*see* Food and Flea Markets). Clothes are another reasonably priced gift item. There are a couple of fashionable boutiques with designer clothes, but the majority of shops stock cotton sportswear and casual resort clothes. Made-to- order clothes are well-made and especially reasonable. Otherwise, be careful, as quality is not high and many goods self-destruct a few months after you get back home.

Shopping

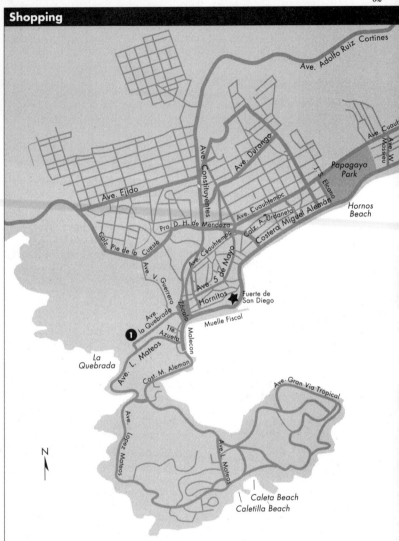

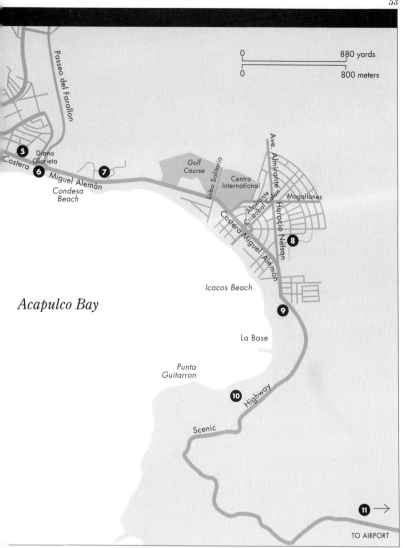

0 | 880 yards
0 | 800 meters

Passeo del Farallon

5 Diana
Glorieta
Costera
6 Miguel Alemán
Condesa
Beach

7

Golf
Course

Centro
International

Ave. Almirante Horacio Nelson

Magallanes

Almirante
Cristobal Colon

8

Lobo Solitario

Costera Miguel Alemán

Acapulco Bay

Icacos Beach

9

La Base

Punta
Guitarron

10 Highway

Scenic

11 →

TO AIRPORT

Shopping Districts

The biggest shopping strip surrounds the Condesa del Mar Hotel and is where you can find Gucci, Acapulco Joe, Pasarela, Istar's, Fiorucci, and others. Downtown (Old) Acapulco doesn't have many name shops, but this is where you'll find the inexpensive tailors patronized by the Mexicans, lots of little souvenir shops, and the "flea" market with crafts made for tourists. The tailors are all on Calle Benito Juárez, just west of the Zócalo. Also in downtown are Woolworth's—which carries the same kinds of goods as in the United States—and a branch of Sanborns, a more upscale place.

Food and Flea Markets

The main market, Mercado Municipal, is described in detail in Exploring.

El Mercado de Artesanías is a five-minute walk from the Zócalo. Turn left as you leave Woolworth's and head straight until you reach the Multibanco Comermex. Turn right for one block and then turn left. When you reach the Banamex, the market is on your right. There are also "fleamarket" signs posted. The market itself is shamelessly inauthentic; everything here is made strictly for foreign consumption, so go just for the amusement. It is a conglomeration of every souvenir in town: fake tribal masks, the ever-present onyx chessboards, the $20 hand-embroidered dress, imitation silver, hammocks, ceramics, even skin cream made from turtles. Don't buy it because turtles are endangered and you won't get it through U.S. Customs. *Open from 10 to 7.* If you don't want to make the trip downtown, try **Noa Noa** on the *Costera at Calle Hurtado de Mendoza*. It's a clean, more commercial version of the Mercado Municipal and also has T-shirts and jewelry, as well as the dozens of souvenirs available in the other markets.

Artesanías Finas de Acapulco (AFA) is one block north of the Costera behind the Baby O disco. Every souvenir you have seen in town and then some are available in 13,000 square feet of air-conditioned shopping space. AFA also carries household items, complete sets of dishes, suitcases, leather goods, conservative clothing, as well as fashionable shorts and T-shirts. The staff is helpful. AFA ships to the United States and accepts major credit cards.

The **Crafts Shop,** in the same building as Taxco El Viejo in La Quebrada before you reach the Mirador Hotel, has not only all the usual crafts but also the best selection of glassware in Acapulco.

Two blocks west of the Zócalo is **Calle José M. Iglesia,** home to a row of little souvenir shops that have a smaller selection than the big markets, but many more T-shirts and more shell sculptures, shell ashtrays, and shell key chains than you ever imagined possible.

Art

The newly opened **Galería de Arte** in the Centro Cultural de Acapulco has a permanent collection of Mexican art as well as exhibits that change about every two weeks. Prices range from $20 to a few hundred. On the Costera near CiCi. *Open 10 AM–1 PM and 5–9 PM. Closed Sun. tel. 4-32-75.*

Galería Rudic, across from the Exelaris Hyatt Continental, is one of the best galleries in town, with a good collection of top contemporary Mexican artists including Armando Amaya, Leonardo Nierman, Norma Goldberg, Trinidad Osorio, José Clemente Orozco, and José David Alfaro Siqueiros. *Open weekdays 10 AM–2 PM and 5–8 PM.*

Galería Victor is the most noteworthy shop in the El Patio shopping center across from the Exelaris Hyatt Continental. On display is the work of Victor Salmones. *Open 10 AM–2 PM and 4–8 PM. Closed Sun.*

The sculptor **Pal Kepenyes** has been receiving good press lately. His jewelry is available in the Exelaris Hyatt Regency arcade. He also displays in his house at Guitarrón 140. Good luck with his perenially busy phone number, tel. 4-47-38.

Sergio Bustamente's whimsical painted papier-mâché and giant ceramic sculptures can be seen at the Princess Hotel shopping arcade and at his own gallery. *Costera Miguel Alemán 711-B, next to American Express.* **El Dorado Gallery,** next door, carries works by his former partner, Mario Gonzáles.

Boutiques

The mall section lists dozens of clothing shops, but there are a few places, mainly near the Condesa del Mar Hotel that are noteworthy. **Mad Max** has tasteful cotton separates in bold colors for children, and shirts sporting the shop's logo (all under $20). **Acapulco Joe, Ruben Torres, Guess,** and **OP** are scattered around the Costera, too. The **Acapulco Joe** seconds shop, La Ganga (The Bargain), is at *Jesus Carranza 11, across from Woolworth's.* The name boutiques' clothes, in varying degrees of quality, are available here for at least half the retail price. Some have only minor irregularities and are therefore a bargain. Back on the Costera at No. 143, are three interconnected shops: **Maria Cantinelli** has mildly dressy clothes for women; **Happy Hour** stocks shirts imprinted with beer and alcohol logos and, in keeping with the appellation, even has a cooler of cold drinks. **Aqua Sport & Casual Wear** has terrific light cotton separates in all colors for around $20. It also has a place to change money and a sports information center. **Daniel Hechter** has just opened a branch near Eve's disco and the Diana Glorieta. There are also a few high-fashion boutiques that will make clothes to order and many can adapt clothes to suit you, so it is always worth asking.

Istar's is at the back of the tiny shopping arcade next to Carlos 'n Charlies. The elegant owner, Sergio, has chic light cotton clothes for men and women. He models his own designs—comfortable summer clothes—with an up-to-date flair. At $40 for men's trousers and $60 for women's dresses, his stock is filled with stylish bargains.

Pasarela, in the Galería Plaza, is a telephone booth-size boutique brimming with lavish costume jewelry and glittering evening dresses all designed in Mexico.

One of **Marietta's** six locations is at the *Princess Hotel arcade*. It has a large collection that ranges from simple daywear to extravagantly sexy party dresses. This is a standby for ex-pats in Acapulco. Though the prices may seem expensive (cotton dresses from $70 to $150), they are quite a bit cheaper than what you would pay in the United States. They also have a good selection of men's shirts.

The **Pitti Palace,** also in the *Princess arcade*, is another bonanza. It is one of the few places carrying sweaters and coats as well as bathing suits and light dresses.

Custom-Made Clothes The most famous of the made-to-order boutiques is **Samy's** at Calle Hidalgo 7, two blocks west of the Zócalo in a little crammed shop next to a florist. The solicitous Spaniard boasts a clientele of international celebrities and many of the important local families. Samy, the charming owner, takes all customers to heart and treats them like old, much-loved friends. He makes clothes for men and women all in light cottons. He can also make costumes, should you be invited to a masquerade party. The patterns are unusual and heavily influenced by Mexican designs, with embroidery and gauze playing a supporting role in the Samy look. The outfits are appropriate for trendy over-30s. Anything that doesn't fit can be altered, and Samy will even work with fabric that you bring in. Prices start at about $25 and go up to about $100.

Esteban's, the most glamorous shop in Acapulco, is on the Costera near the Club de Golf. Like Samy, he will make clothes to order and adapt anything you see in the shop. The similarity ends there. Esteban's clothes are far more formal and fashionable. His opulent evening dresses range from $200 to $1,000, though daytime dresses average $85. If you scour the racks, you can find something for $60. He stocks very skimpy bathing suits, accessories, and quality sportswear for both men and women. Esteban has a back room of designer clothes.

Jewelry

The newly opened **Aha,** on the *Costera next to the Crazy Lobster*, has the most unusual costume jewelry in Acapulco. Designed by owner Cecilia Rodriguez, this is really campy, colorful stuff that is bound to attract attention. Prices range from $12 to $300.

Emi Fors are tony jewelry shops owned by Mrs. Fors, a former Los Angelean. The stores stock gold, silver, and some semiprecious stones. Three branches: *Galería Plaza*, the *Exelaris Hyatt Continental*, and the *Calinda Quality Inn*.

Leather

Leather goods are inexpensive in Mexico but generally not of the highest quality. Some articles are liable to fall apart a few months after you get them home, so shop carefully and don't plan to buy anything to pass on to your grandchildren. Best bets for quality are Gucci and Aries. **Gucci** sells leather shoes and accessories in Mexican versions of Italian designs that are much-loved by fashionable Mexicans. It is a good place for men's shoes, and the prices are reasonable considering the cachet of a Gucci item. Women's handbags range from $70 to $150. Costera 102 near El Presidente, across from the Exelaris Hyatt Continental, at La Vista Mall, the Exelaris Hyatt Regency, and the Acapulco Plaza. *Open from 10 AM–2 PM and 5–9 PM.*

Aries, the other reputable leather goods dealer in Acapulco, sells pieces made from Mexican leather sent to Spain to be cured, then returned to Mexico to be fashioned into luggage, handbags, and briefcases. Prices are a bit less than at Gucci's but not substantially lower. Las Brisas Hotel, in La Vista Mall and at the Acapulco Plaza.

Silver

Many people come to Mexico to buy silver. Taxco, three hours away, is one of the leading silver capitals of the world. Prices in Acapulco are lower than in the United States but not dirt-cheap by any means. Bangles start at $8 and go up to $20; bracelets range from $20 to $60. Just look out for the 9.25 sterling silver hallmark, or buy the more inexpensive silver plate that is dipped in several coats *(baños)* of silver. **Antonio Pineda** and the **Castillo Brothers** are two of the more famous design names. Designs range from traditional bulky necklaces (often made with turquoise) to streamlined bangles and chunky earrings. Not much flatware can be found, although Emi Fors and Taxco El Viejo do carry some.

Taxco El Viejo, in a large colonial building in Old Acapulco, has the largest silver selection in Acapulco. Pieces seen all over town crop up here as well as more unusual designs. Also for sale are flatware and a large range of ornamental belt buckles. If you buy several pieces, you can request a discount. Beware of heavy-handed sales techniques such as offering to send a taxi to pick you up at your hotel, a tactic meant to make you feel obligated to buy something. *La Quebrada 830.*

Joya, a new addition to the Acapulco Plaza, stocks a good collection of inexpensive silver jewelry in modern designs, and an extensive array of low-priced bangles (in the $6 range). Joya even stocks children's sizes. To top it off, Joya sells wholesale and will give a 30% discount on every item. A perfect place to pick up gifts.

Pineda de Taxco, Acapulco Plaza, has a glittering display of silver jewelry sold by weight. The 20% discount saves you the tax and then some. *Open Mon.–Sat. 9–9.*

Pupu, Acapulco Princess shopping center, carries pieces by Castillo and Pineda and a small collection of simple but elegant jewelry.

Malls

Malls are all the rage in Acapulco and are constantly being built. These range from the lavish air-conditioned shopping arcade at the Princess to rather gloomy collections of shops that sell cheap jewelry and embroidered dresses. Malls are listed below from east to west.

The **Princess's** cool arcade is Acapulco's classiest and most comfortable mall. Best bets are quality jewelry, clothes, accessories, and artwork. Even if you are staying on The Strip, it is worth the cab ride out here just to see the shops: *Dudu* offers a wide range of leather, trinkets for the house, and silver jewelry; *Pitti* carries women's clothes—jackets and coats and Mexican-accented dresses for $250, and casual daywear in the $150 range; *Aca Joe* and *Fiorucci* have branches here as does *Ronay* jewelers. *Marietta* has a large collection of men's and women's clothes. One of Sergio Bustamente's galleries is at the Princess along with **La Vista.** Serious shopping takes place at this East Bay collection of boutiques designed as a Mexican village. *Benny's* has a good choice of sportswear for men and women. *Aries* and *Gucci* have the best selection of quality leather in Acapulco. *Thelma's* stocks both ready-to-wear and made-to-order ladies' fashions. A new shop, *Benamy*, has a terrific range of silver jewelry. *Marietta* is crammed with accessories and dresses influenced by Mexican designs.

Plaza Icacos, at the bottom of the hill, has a few shops and Regine's restaurant upstairs. Across from the Condesa del Mar Hotel is the **Plaza Condesa,** which offers a cold-drink stand, an Italian restaurant, a weight-training center, and more silver shops per square foot than anywhere in Acapulco. Next door to Plaza Condesa is a high-tech, two-story building with *Jag', Goldie,* and *OP* for trendy sportswear; opulent *Pasarela's; Rubén Torres;* and *Acapulco Joe.* Two branches of *Mad Max* carrying children's inexpensive unisex clothes in basic colored cotton are here, too. The multilevel **Marbella Mall,** at the Diana Glorieta, opened in April 1988 with a branch of Nike and Ellesse (logo sports clothes and tennis outfits). *Marti,* which has every single piece of sports equipment you could ever need is here also. **El Patio,** across from the Exelaris Hyatt Continental, has two recommendable art galleries and a fairly generic collection of clothing and silver shops.

Galería Acapulco Plaza is a new two-story structure of lusciously air-conditioned shops built around a courtyard. Except for silver, you could find many similar items at home. But this is a good place to pick up some cotton sportswear or a pretty dress to wear to a disco. Any self-respecting child would love a Disney-character sweatshirt or T-shirt from *Patrick Jordan.* For fancier duds, *Faian Vergona* and *Pasarela* do a line of locally designed glitzy evening dresses. *Pasarela* also carries chunky, *diamante* jewelry. The only truly Mexican souvenirs can be found in the *Pineda de Taxco* jewelry shop and in one small folk art shop. *Guess* is one block west as you leave the plaza. Across from the plaza is the **Flamboyant Mall,** similar in style to El Patio.

Department Stores

Sanborns is the most non-Mexican of the big shops. It sells English-language newspapers, magazines, and books as well as a line of high-priced souvenirs, but its Mexican glassware and ceramics cannot be found anywhere else in town. This is a useful place to come for postcards, cosmetics, and medicines. Sanborns restaurants are recommended for glorified coffee-shop food. The branch adjacent to the Condesa, *Costera Miguel Alemán 209, is open until 1 AM; the downtown branch, Costera Miguel Alemán 1206, closes at 11 PM.*

Super-Super and **Gigante,** both on the Costera near Papagayo Park, sell one of everything from light bulbs and newspapers to bottles of tequila and postcards. If you are missing anything at all, you should be able to pick it up at either of these stores or at the **Commercial Mexicana,** a store a little closer to The Strip. *Open until 9 PM.*

Woolworth's, corner of Escudero and Matamora Streets in Old Acapulco, is much like the five-and-dime found all over the United States, but with a Mexican feel. You can purchase American brands of shampoo for less than they cost at home, as well as paper goods, cheap clothes, handmade children's toys, and the ubiquitous Acapulco shell ashtrays. *Open until 9 PM.*

6 Sports and Fitness

Participant Sports and Fitness

Acapulco has lots for sports lovers to enjoy. Most hotels have pools, and there are several tennis courts on The Strip. The weight-training craze is beginning to catch on and the first gyms are opening. You'll find one at Plaza Condesa across from the Condesa del Mar Hotel.

Fishing Sailfish, marlin, shark, and mahimahi are the usual catches. Head down to the docks near the Zócalo and see just how many people offer to take you out for $20 a day. It is safer to stick with one of the reliable companies with boats and equipment in good condition.

Fishing boats can be arranged through your hotel, downtown at the Pesca Deportiva near the *muelle* (dock) across from the Zócalo, or through travel agents. Boats accommodating four to eight people run $200–$250 a day. Excursions usually leave about 7 AM and return at 2 PM. You are required to get a license ($2) from the Secretaría de Pesca above the central post office downtown. Don't show up during siesta, between 2 and 4 in the afternoon. Small boats for freshwater fishing can be rented at Cadena's and Tres Marías at Coyuca lagoon.

Fitness Acapulco is a tropical resort with year-round weather that is like August in the warmest parts of the United States. This means that you should cut back on your workouts and maintain proper hydration by drinking plenty of water.

Acapulco Princess Hotel (Carretera Escénica, Km. 17, tel. 748/43–100) offers the best fitness facilities, with eight pools, 16 tennis courts—including two that are indoors *and* air-conditioned—and a gym with stationary bikes, Universal machines, and free weights. The Princess and its sister hotel, the Pierre Marqués, share two beautifully maintained, 18-hole golf courses. Golf clubs are available to rent. Because the Princess is about nine miles from the city center, you can even swim in the ocean here and still avoid the pollution of Acapulco Bay.

Westin Las Brisas (Carretera Escénica 5255, tel. 748/4–15–80) is the place to stay if you like to swim but don't like company or competition. Individual *casitas*, or bungalows, come with private, or semiprivate, pools, and the views of the bay are stunning from pools and terraces here.

Most of the major hotels in town along the Costera Miguel Alemán also have pools, which is where you should do your swimming. In spite of the city's recent efforts to clean up Acapulco Bay, the sea opposite the city center is still to be avoided.

Golf There are two 18-hole championship golf courses shared by the Princess and Pierre Marqués hotels. Reservations should be made in advance (tel. 4–31–00). Greens fees are $31 for guests and $41 for non-guests. There is also a public golf course at the Clubs de Golf on The Strip across from Elcano Hotel. Greens fees for nine holes are $10; $20 for 18 holes (tel. 4–07–81).

Horseback Riding This activity is available at Revolcadero as well as Barra Vieja for as little as $3 an hour. Check at your hotel's activities desk.

Jogging As in Mexico City, visiting gringos and several world-class Mexican runners have ensured that jogging has caught on here among all classes of people. The only real venue for running in the downtown area, however, is along the sidewalk next to the seafront Costera Miguel Alemán. Early morning is the best time, since traffic is heavy along this thoroughfare during most of the day. End to end it measures close to seven miles, although your hotel will probably lie somewhere in the middle of the route. The beach is another option but, like beaches everywhere, the going is tough with soft sand and sloping contours. Away from the city center, the best area for running is out at the Acapulco Princess Hotel, on the airport road. A two-km loop (1.2 mi) is laid out along a lightly traveled road and, in the early morning, you can also run along the asphalt trails on the golf course.

Scuba Diving **Divers de México,** owned by a helpful and efficient American woman, features English-speaking captains and comfortable American-built yachts. A four-hour scuba diving excursion including equipment, lessons in a pool for beginners, lunch, and drinks costs $50 per person. If you are a certified diver, the excursion is $40; if you bring your own equipment, it is $30. Equipment is available for underwater photography, and pickups from most hotels can be arranged. Divers de México also rents chairs on fishing boats and runs three-hour sunset champagne cruises to watch the cliff divers (tel. 2–13–98 or 3–60–20).

Arnold Brothers also runs daily scuba excursions and snorkeling trips. The scuba trips cost U.S. $45 and last for 2½ hours.

Tennis Court prices range from about $14 to $20 an hour during the day, and are $2–$3 more in the evening. Non-hotel guests pay about $5 more per hour. Lessons, with English-speaking instructors, are about $25 an hour; ball boys get a $2 tip.

Acapulco Plaza, 4 clay courts, 3 lighted for evening play (tel. 4–80–50).
Acapulco Princess, 2 indoor courts, 6 outdoor (tel. 4–31–00).
Club de Tennis and Golf, across from Hotel Malibu, Costera Miguel Alemán (tel. 4–48–24).
Exelaris Hyatt Continental, 2 lighted courts (tel. 4–09–09).
Exelaris Hyatt Regency, 4 lighted courts (tel. 4–12–25).
Pierre Marqués, 8 courts (tel. 4–20–00).
Tiffany's Racquet Club, Avenue Villa Vera 120, 5 courts (tel. 4–79–49).
Villa Vera Hotel, 3 outdoor lighted clay courts (tel. 4–03–33).

Water Sports Waterskiing, broncos (one-person motor boats), and parasailing can all be arranged on the beach. Parasailing is an Acapulco highlight and looks terrifying until you actually try it. Most people who do it love the view and go back again and again. An eight-minute trip costs $10 (tel. 2–20–56, 2–13–78). Waterskiing is about $25 an hour; broncos cost $15 an hour. Windsurfing can be organized at **El Colonial** across from Fort San Diego (tel. 3–70–77). The main surfing beach is Revolcadero.

Spectator Sports

Bullfights The season runs from December to Easter, Sundays at 5:30 PM. Tickets are available through your hotel or from Motel Kennedy behind Botas Moy along The Strip or at the Plaza de Toros ticket window (open Mon.–Sat. 10–2 and Sun. 10:30–3). Tickets cost from $7.50 to $10, and a seat in the shade (*sombra*) is worth the extra cost. Also check the local paper and signs around town to find out if any noteworthy matadors can be seen in action (tel. 5–85–40).

7 Dining

Introduction

Dining in Acapulco is more than just eating out—it is the most popular leisure activity in town. Every night the restaurants fill up, and every night the adventurous diner can sample a different cuisine: Italian, German, Japanese, American, Tex-Mex, and, of course, plain old Mex. The variety of styles matches the range of cuisines: from greasy spoons that serve regional specialties to roof-top gourmet restaurants with gorgeous views of Acapulco Bay. Most restaurants fall somewhere in the middle, and on The Strip there are dozens of palapa-roof beachside restaurants, as well as wildly decorated rib and hamburger joints popular with visitors under 30.

One plus for Acapulco dining is that the food is garden-fresh. Each morning the Mercado Municipal is abuzz with restaurant managers and locals buying up the vegetables that will appear on plates that evening. Mexican beef, however, is not up to U.S. standards and all tourist restaurants get their beef from the same producer—don't believe anyone's claim that his steak or hamburgers have been imported from the United States. All the restaurants use the same ingredients, and the following dishes are Mexican menu staples:

Caldo Rojo. A spicy red chicken broth filled with rice, chickpeas, carrots, zucchini, chicken, avocado, and cilantro (coriander). This hearty dish is found only in authentic Mexican restaurants.
Camarones. These jumbo shrimp, though not caught in Acapulco, are tender if cooked right.
Ceviche. Don't pass up this popular appetizer said to have originated in Acapulco. It is raw shellfish or white fish fillets marinated in lime juice and is a light cocktail before any meal.
Guacamole. The Mexican version often includes onions, cilantro, tomatoes and a generous amount of *chiles serranas*, making this avocado dip much spicier than the U.S. equivalent.
Huachinango. This locally caught red snapper is usually served whole or in boned fillets. It is a mild fish and very filling whether grilled or prepared in a light garlic sauce.
Langosta. This lobster is also fresh though not caught in the bay. It is more expensive and less meaty than its Atlantic relations.
Pozole. This thick hominy soup with nuggets of pork is found only in Mexican establishments.
Tortillas. A staple of the Mexican diet, these thin rounds of corn soaked in lime, then salted, form the basis of enchiladas, tacos, and tostadas. In many restaurants, tortillas are served on the side instead of bread.

Establishments that cater to tourists purify their drinking water and use it to cook vegetables. In smaller restaurants, ask for bottled water with or without bubbles (*con* or *sin gas*); the brand often served is Tehuácan; or just ask for *agua mineral* to receive a bottle of club soda. The usual rules apply at the local restaurants: eat only cooked vegetables, and no matter where you are, it is sensible to peel all fruit. The small stands on the street serve inexpensive, filling food—a plate of tacos usually costs between 50¢ and $1. But before you eat, look around to note the fly count. Contrary to popular belief, most Mexican dishes are not *picante* (spicy). Chili sauces are served in bowls on the side so you can adjust the spiciness to your taste; the

Dining

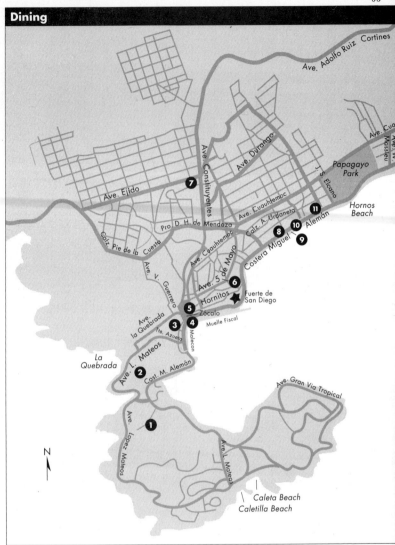

Antojito's Mayab, **11**
Barbarroja, **17**
Bella Italia, **10**
Beto's, **21**

Blackbeard's, **20**
Carlos 'n Charlies, **22**
Coyuca 22, **1**
Crazy Lobster, **16**
D'Joint, **26**

El Real, **23**
Embarcadero, **27**
Goyo's, **6**
Hard Times, **25**

Le Gourmet, **34**
Los Rancheros, **29**
Madeiras, **33**
Maximilian's, **14**
Mimi's Chili Saloon, **19**

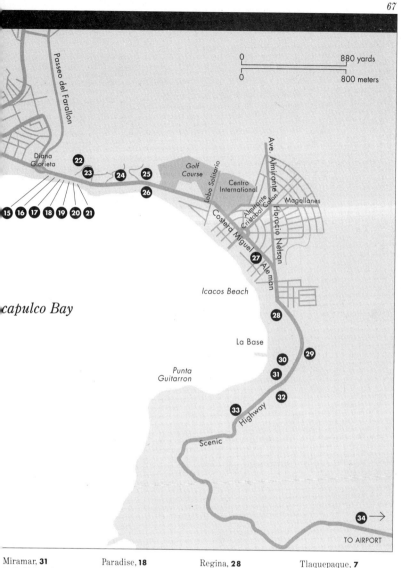

0　　　　　　880 yards
0　　　　　　800 meters

Passeo del Farallon

Diana
Glorieta

Golf
Course

Centro
International

Ave. Almirante

Almirante Cristobal Colon

Horacio Nelson

Magallanes

Lobo Solitario

Costera Miguel Aleman

Icacos Beach

capulco Bay

La Base

Punta
Guitarron

Highway

Scenic

TO AIRPORT

22
23 24 25
26
15 16 17 18 19 20 21
27
28
30 29
31
32
33
34 →

green chili sauce adds a mild tang, but the red is very strong and should be approached with care. Most hotels have breakfast buffets; in restaurants you'll have a choice of sweet rolls and coffee, fruit salad, pancakes, or *huevos rancheros* (fried eggs on a tortilla, with spicy tomato sauce). Manzanilla, an herbal tea, is served. Mexicans eat breakfast at any time in the morning. Lunch, the main meal of the day, is served from 2 to 4 PM. Dinner is late by American standards, and many restaurants don't get crowded until about 9, leaving less time to kill if you are planning to hit the discos later.

Service is usually good but often slow. Most waiters and managers have been in the business for a long time and take pride in what they do. One advantage to slow service is that restaurants don't close until the last customer has left, so it is easy to enjoy a meal at leisure. Tipping is optional in the more informal restaurants, but otherwise 10% to 15% is correct.

Mexican wine is pretty bad and drinking it with dinner adds to the cost. But cocktails are an Acapulco specialty, and some restaurants serve as many different drinks as they have dishes. (For a complete discussion on imbibing in Mexico, see Nightlife.)

Health food has finally hit. The Villa Vera has diet lunch platters and there are numerous cafés that have fruit shakes and fruit salad platters. In the Tex/Mex and American restaurants, you can often find a big salad bar loaded with fresh vegetables.

The top restaurants in Acapulco can be fun for a splurge and provide very good value. Even at the best places in town dinner rarely exceeds $35 per person, and the atmosphere and views are fantastic. Ties and jackets are out of place, but so are shorts or jeans. You may have to taxi back to your hotel to change. Gourmets and epicures are warned: haute cuisine is not to be found. Although the food is fresh, and carefully prepared, it does not compare with what is available in Europe or in large North American cities. Ordering something that is not produced locally is asking for trouble. Asparagus, for example, is often canned, artichokes are usually not up to scratch, and many chefs have not mastered the art of preparing a truly subtle sauce. Reservations are advised for all restaurants in the very expensive and expensive categories. Unless stated all are open daily from 6:30 or 7 PM until the last diner leaves.

Highly recommended restaurants in each price category are indicated by a star ★.

Category	Cost*
Very Expensive	$50 and up
Expensive	$25–$50
Moderate	$10–$25
Inexpensive	Under $10

* *per person excluding drinks, service, and sales tax (15%)*

Very Expensive

French Le Gourmet. Although its food is wildly inconsistent, this restaurant, in the Acapulco Princess hotel, is thought by many to be one of Acapulco's premier establishments. Many people staying down on the Costera brave the 15-minute taxi ride to partake of a tranquil meal in a plush setting. The French menu has all the classics: vichyssoise, steak au poivre sautéed in cognac, and such Acapulco favorites as lobster and red snapper fillets. The atmosphere is luxurious and genteel, with roomy, comfortable chairs, silent waiters, and air-conditioning. *Acapulco Princess Hotel, tel. 748/4–31–00. AE, DC, MC, V.*

Gourmet **Coyuca 22.** This is possibly the most expensive restaurant in Acapulco; it is certainly one of the most beautiful. Entering Coyuca is like walking onto a film set. Diners eat on terraces that overlook the bay from the west, on a hilltop in Old Acapulco. The understated decor consists of Doric pillars, sculptures, and large onyx flower stands near the entrance. Diners gaze down on an enormous illuminated obelisk and a small pool. The effect is like eating in a partially restored Greek ruin sans dust. The tiny menu centers on seafood with lobster the house specialty. Prime rib is also available. *Avenida Coyuca 22, (a 10-minute taxi ride southwest of the Zócalo), tel. 748/2–34–68 or 3–50–30. AE, DC, MC, V. Closed Apr. 30–Nov. 1.*

Expensive

American **Embarcadero.** A nautical motif pervades Embarcadero, which is well-loved by both Acapulco regulars and resident Americans. It is designed to look like a wharf with the bar as the loading office. Wooden bridges lead past a fountain to the thatched eating area, piled high with wood on packing crates and maps. The food is American with a Polynesian touch. You can have deep fried shrimps with soy sauce, chicken, or steak. The "salad barge" is enormous. *Costera Miguel Alemán, west of CiCi Park, tel. 748/4–87–87. Open 6 PM–midnight. Reservations not accepted. AE, DC, MC, V. Closed Mon. out of season.*

Continental **Maximilian's.** An exception to the rule that says hotels don't serve top-quality food is this Acapulco Plaza restaurant. A haven for American expatriates who like to dress up and come for a treat, it is the only beachside restaurant with air-conditioning. Lobster, duck, and seafood cooked with classic ingredients are the specialties, and steak is available, too. *Acapulco Plaza, tel. 748/5–80–50. AE, DC, MC, V.*

Regina. One of the more recent additions to Acapulco's elite dining roster, Regina's had an instant following. Air-conditioned and elegant—in a quasi-French manner—the place has a European feel. Ambitious Continental describes the menu, which includes oysters Rockefeller with Pernod (in season), lobster bisque, and chicken Kiev. Of note is Pescado Regina, fresh fish stuffed with asparagus. *Plaza Icacos, tel. 748/4–86–53. AE, MC, V.*

French **El Real.** A new kid on the block, El Real has already set up house ★ as one of Acapulco's best. The setting is unlike any in Acapulco: an antique-filled dining room and bar within a complex of four restaurants and a military museum—all this in a building designed to look like an 18th-century fort. Lavish floral arrangements decorate the entrance to the dining area, and high, wooden booths ensure intimate meals. Several private rooms are also available for small groups, as is the lusciously cool wine cellar. French chef Roger Bergeret Decrevel produces some of the best food in Acapulco by melding the cuisines of Mexico and France. Octopus stew in cognac, and oysters and red snapper baked in pastry are some of the specialties, but beef lovers also will find a healthy selection. *El Fuerte del Virrey, Roca Sol 17, Club Deportivo (behind Carlos 'n Charlies), tel. 748/4–33–21. AE, DC, MC, V. Closed Mon.*

★ **Miramar.** Lightwood furniture and a fountain provide the decoration for this understated place, but the real glamour comes from the view of the bay and the flickering lights of Acapulco. Traditional dishes, like pâté and lobster thermidor, are served alongside classics with a new twist: ceviche with a hint of coconut, and red snapper papillote. Shrimp mousse and duck are both specialties. Miramar is not as intimate as its neighbor, Madeiras, and many large groups from the Princess book long tables, so the noise level is rather high. *Scenic Highway, tel. 748/4–75–74. AE, MC, V.*

Seafood **Barbarroja.** Eating at this outdoor restaurant is very much like sitting on the deck of a ship. A large mast does virtually nothing to block the view of the street, so don't bother coming here if you want privacy. The crowd is older, as the calm atmosphere and relatively high prices discourage those under 30. This is a good place for seafood: lobster tail with filet mignon is the house specialty, which comes with a bottle of Mexican wine or an after-dinner drink. Steer clear of the ice-cold, but tasteless, strawberry daiquiris. *Costera Miguel Alemán, next to Mimi's Chili Saloon. No telephone. AE, DC, MC, V.*

Moderate

American **Carlos 'n Charlies.** Without a doubt the most popular restau-
★ rant in town, a line forms well before the 6:30 PM opening. Part of the Anderson group (with restaurants in the United States and Spain, as well as Mexico), Carlos 'n Charlies cultivates an atmosphere of controlled craziness. Prankster waiters, a joke-ster menu, and eclectic decor—everything from antique bullfight photos to a veritable tool chest of painted gadgets hanging from the ceiling—add to the chaos. The crowd is mostly young and relaxed—which is what you need to be to put up with the rush-hour traffic noise that filters up to the covered balcony where people dine. The menu straddles the border, with ribs, stuffed shrimp, and oysters among the best offerings. *Costera Miguel Alemán, tel. 748/4–12–85 or 4–00–39. Reservations not accepted. AE, DC, MC, V.*

D'Joint. Locals as well as tourists love D'Joint—a claustrophobic restaurant with a funky, publike atmosphere—so, in season, prepare for a wait. In addition to the usual steaks, salads, and nachos, prime ribs are the house specialty. The four types of roast beef sandwiches are a hit but not between 8 and 11, when only dinner is served. After your meal, try "sexy coffee," cappuccino with liqueur. *Costera Miguel Alemán, next to Calinda Quality Inn, tel. 748/4–37–09. Reservations not accepted. AE, DC, MC, V. Closed one week in summer.*

Pepe and Co. Next door to Carlos 'n Charlies, Pepe and Co. is owned by Pepe Valle. Many of the waiters and waitresses are Carlos 'n Charlies alumni, and Pepe's has the atmosphere of a place for C' n C customers who've hit 30. Dark wood walls and dim lights set the tone; Pepe's is a tad more formal than other places on The Strip in the same price range. Lobster and *filete* *boccacio*—steak smothered in a cheese sauce—are the house dishes. After dinner many repair to the smoky piano bar. *Costera Miguel Alemán, next to Carlos 'n Charlies, tel. 478/4–70–88. No reservations. AE, DC, MC, V.*

Sanborns. Both branches of this all-purpose store have dining rooms. The food is basic coffee-shop fare, with an extensive all-day breakfast menu offering steak, shrimp, and an enormous array of baked goods. Sanborns on the Costera has the best American coffee around and a terrace with a view of the bay. In the mornings, sit under the canopy or on the left side of the patio to avoid the sun. *Costera Miguel Alemán, next to Condesa del Mar hotel, tel. 748/4–44–65; next to the post office in Old Acapulco. No reservations. AE, MC, V.*

Continental **Madeiras.** Vying with neighbor Miramar for "most chichi place in Acapulco," there are fierce arguments as to which has the best food. Madeiras is very difficult to get into; many people make reservations by letter before their arrival. At the very least, call the minute you get to Acapulco. Children under 12 are not welcome, however. All the tables at Madeiras have a view of glittering Acapulco by night. The furniture is certainly unusual: the spacious bar/reception area has art nouveau–style carved chairs, plump sofas, and startling coffee tables made of glass resting on large wooden animals. All the dishes and silverware were created by silversmiths in the nearby town of Taxco. Dinner is served from a four-course, prix fixe menu and costs about $20 without wine. Entrées include the delicious Spanish dish of red snapper in sea salt, tasty chilled soups, stuffed red snapper, and a choice of steaks and other seafood. The *crepas de chuitlacoche* (corn-fungus crêpes) are a Mexican specialty, served by the Aztecs. Desserts are competently prepared but have no special flair. There are two seatings, at 7:30 and 10:30. Unfortunately, diners coming at the later time may find selections limited. *Scenic Highway, tel. 748/4–73–16. AE, DC, MC, V. Closed Sun.*

★ **Pinzona 65.** Benny Hudson, a Mexican with years of hotel and catering experience in Acapulco and around the world, is the proprietor of this new restaurant, and it looks to be a winner. On a rooftop in the old part of town, Pinzona 65 is perfect for open-air dining with a view. All the food is served on custom made ceramic dishes that feature a drawing of the enormous chandelier in the entrance. Quality beef and the catch of the day highlight the menu. Especially worthwhile is callaco, red snapper simmered in a light garlic sauce and garnished with pineapple and banana. The food is unpretentious and well-prepared and some of the best in town. *Pinzona 65, a five-minute drive northwest of Zócalo, tel. 748/3–03–88. Reservations advised on weekends. DC, MC, V.*

French **Normandie.** Recognized as the only authentic French restaurant in town, this small place is run by the charming Madame Chauvin and her daughter. The Normandie has pastel blue walls and a little fountain reminiscent of a Parisian tearoom, and the platters of cakes near the door add to this impression. The menu touches all bases including beef bourguignon and seafood gratinée. Even early in the season it's packed with customers and rushed waiters, so reservations are a must. *On the Costera near the Super-Super, tel. 748/5–19–16. AE, DC, MC, V. Closed May 1–Nov. 1.*

Mexican **Pancho's.** The only source for Mexican food right on the beach, Pancho's is open for lunch and dinner. During the day you get a free drink with your meal. Though the food is good, the selection is rather generic. *Costera Miguel Alemán, next to Crazy Lobster, tel. 748/4-10-96. AE, DC, MC, V.*

Mixed Menu **Hard Times.** With an unusually large menu for Acapulco,
★ Hard Times features the usual Tex-Mex dishes as well as plenty of barbecue, fresh fish, and the largest salad bar in town. The dining area is an attractive open terrace, with a partial view of the bay. Although right in the center of The Strip, Hard Times is a tranquil haven—decorated with palms and incandescent lights—in which to enjoy generous portions of American food and, sometimes, music provided by the resident DJ. Arrive early; there is often a wait in high season. *Costera Miguel Alemán, across from the Calinda Quality Inn (look for the red neon lights), tel. 784/4-00-64. Reservations not accepted. AE, DC, MC, V. Closed Sun.*

Seafood **Beto's.** By day, you can eat right on the beach and enjoy live music; by night, this palapa-roofed restaurant is transformed into a dim and romantic dining area lighted by candles and paper lanterns. Whole red snapper, lobster, and ceviche are recommended. *Costera Miguel Alemán, tel. 748/4-04-73. Reservations advised. AE, DC, MC, V.*

★ **Blackbeard's.** A dark, glorified coffee shop with a pirate ship motif, Blackbeard's has maps covering the tables in the cozy booths, and the walls are adorned with wooden figureheads. Every movie star from Bing Crosby to Liz Taylor who ever stepped foot here has his/her photo posted in the lounge. A luscious salad bar and jumbo portions of shrimp, steak, and lobster keep customers satisfied; owned by the proprietors of Mimi's Chili Saloon. *Costera Miguel Alemán, tel. 748/4-25-49. Reservations not accepted. AE, DC, MC, V.*

Crazy Lobster. Sharing owners with Beto's, Crazy Lobster also shares appearance: a palapa roof outside but hanging plants and a big tank of tropical fish within. Every night except Monday, live music provides a soft background to the quick and friendly service. Broiled lobster and shrimp are the specialties. *Costera Miguel Alemán, next to Paradise, tel. 748/4-59-74. Reservations not necessary. AE, MC, V.*

Paradise. This is the leading beach-party restaurant. Hawaiian-shirted waiters drop leis over your head as you arrive and hand roses to the ladies. The menu (primarily seafood) has the same number of dishes as drinks, a pretty good indicator of what this place is like. Paradise has one of the biggest dance floors in Acapulco and live music day and night. Chaos reigns at lunchtime (from 2 to 5), and the mood picks up again from 8:30 to 10:30. Expect a young crowd. *Costera Miguel Alemán, next to Mimi's Chili Saloon, tel. 748/4-59-88. No reservations. AE, DC, MC, V.*

Spanish **Parador.** Part of a chain with branches in Canada, the United States, Spain, and Mexico City, this light, spacious restaurant has a fantastic view of the bay. Specialties include tapas and award-winning paella, made with pasta instead of rice. *La Vista shopping complex, Scenic Highway, tel. 748/4-80-20. Reservations advised on weekends. AE, DC, MC, V.*

Sirocco. This beachside eatery is numero uno for those who crave Spanish food in Acapulco. The tile floors and heavy wooden furniture give it a Mediterranean feel. Specialties include *pulpo en su tinta* (octopus in its own ink) and 10 varieties of fresh fish. Order paella when you arrive at the beach—it takes a half hour to prepare. *Costera Miguel Alemán, across from Super-Super, tel. 748/2–10–30. No reservations. AE, DC, MC, V.*

Tex-Mex **Palenque.** Opened in mid-April 1988, it is too early to tell how Palenque (across from the Fantasy disco) will fare, but one thing is certain—it will be the spot for spectacular dining. More than $3 million was spent on this huge place seating 700. Every night diners will witness traditional folk dances, cockfights, and the Flying Indians of Papantla. A more secluded area will accommodate those wanting to eat without seeing the show. Menu: Tex-Mex plus steak, chicken, and fish. *On the Scenic Highway; no phone, credit card information, or hours at press time.*

Inexpensive

American **Woolworth's.** The Old Acapulco branch has an air-conditioned coffee shop with a large menu of Mexican and American food. If you get a sudden urge for a BLT or hot fudge sundae, come here. *Next to Sanborns downtown.*

Health Food **100% Natural.** Six family-operated restaurants specialize
★ in light, healthful food—yogurt shakes, fruit salads, and sandwiches made with wholewheat bread. The service is quick and the food is a refreshing alternative to tacos, particularly on a hot day. Look for the green signs with white lettering. *Costera Miguel Alemán 204, near the Acapulco Plaza. No phone or credit cards. Another branch is near the Acapulco Princess.*

Italian **Bella Italia.** For more than 20 years Bella Italia has been run by
★ an Italian family. Although old-time Acapulqueños claim the food is not what it once was, it is still very good, and there's always a crowd partaking of the many pasta dishes served with a basket of crispy hot rolls in a cool palapa-roof hut overlooking the ocean. The clam sauce is superb. *Costera Miguel Alemán, opposite Hotel El Cid, (a five-minute taxi ride from The Strip), tel. 748/5–17–57. No reservations or credit cards.*

Mexican **Antojito's Mayab.** From the exterior, this place is offputting. It looks like a cross between a flea market and a circus. Neon lights, striped walls, a portrait of Christ, dead plants, and Mayan-style paintings are all casually flung together. But this open-air restaurant is conveniently located on the Costera, though the hubbub of the traffic can be annoying. There is a large variety of Yucatán dishes, many for only $5. This is about as untouristy as Acapulco gets. The *tablita*, a combination of smoked, dried, pickled, and grilled meats, is enormous. The crusty enchiladas and Yucatán tamales are favorites, though they bear little resemblance to Tex-Mex. *Costera Miguel Alemán, next to Super-Super, tel. 748/5–24–14. AE, DC, MC, V.*
★ **Goyo's.** Card tables and rickety chairs make Goyo's fine cooking a complete surprise. Customers are primarily Mexican, though many Canadians and Europeans find their way here, too. The staff is uniformly friendly and efficient and specials such as steaks, chicken enchiladas, and filet mignon wrapped in bacon arrive in an instant. Breakfast offerings are generous and eco-

nomical. *Calle Cinco de Mayo at the corner of Calle Dos de Abril. No phone. No credit cards.*

Los Rancheros. With a view of the water in the posh East Bay, here's Mexican food at about half what you'd pay at Madeiras or Miramar. The decor is colorful, folksy Mexican with paper streamers, checked tablecloths, and lopsided mannequins in local dress. Some say the quality of the food has slipped with the new management, so come for drinks only if you don't want to be disappointed. There are two menus: one for Mexicans and a higher-priced one for tourists. Make sure you get the former if you want the real thing. Specials include *carne tampiqueña* (fillet of beef broiled with lemon juice), chicken enchiladas, and *queso fundido* (melted cheese served as a side dish to chips). *Scenic Highway, tel. 748/4–19–08. AE, MC, V.*

Restaurant San Carlos. Ignore the café atmosphere and Woolworth school-of-art paintings on the walls of Restaurant San Carlos. Pay attention instead to the barbecued meats grilled at your table in this patio/dining room, half a block west of the Zócalo. Beer only. *Calle Benito Juárez 5, tel. 748/264–59. MC, V.*

★ **Tlaquepaque.** As hard to find as it is to pronounce, this is one of the best restaurants in Acapulco. It's well worth the 15-minute cab ride into the northwestern residential section of Acapulco (tell your driver it is around the corner from the Oficina de Tránsito). Owner/chef José Arreola was a chef at the Pierre Marqués for 15 years and he takes his job very seriously. Don't insult him by asking if the water is purified or if the vegetables are safe. The menu is limited but excellent and authentic. If your party numbers four or more, Señor Arreola likes nothing better than to select a family-style meal, which can include quail liver tostadas, deep fried tortillas, and *chiles rellenos*. The alfresco dining area sits on a stone terrace bordered by pink flowering bushes and an abandoned well. The outside tables have a perfect view of the kitchen filled with locally made pots. Thursday is pozole day, when a thick soup of hominy and pork is served. *Calle Uno, Lote 7, Colonia Vista Alegre, tel. 748/5–70–55. Cash only.*

★ **Zorrito's.** For years locals have known about Zorrito's (across from the Plaza), a rather dingy café that fills up with partygoers snacking between discos. A spanking new, very clean restaurant of the same name is already attracting tourists. The menu features a host of steak and beef dishes, and the special, *filete tampiqueña*, comes with tacos, enchiladas, guacamole, and frijoles. *Costera Miguel Alemán, next to Botas Moy, tel. 748/5–37–35. MC, V.*

Popular **Mimi's Chili Saloon.** Right next door to Barbarroja's is this two-
★ level, wooden restaurant decorated with everything from Marilyn Monroe posters to cages of tropical birds and a collection of ridiculous signs. It's frequented by those under 30 who gorge on Tex-Mex, onion rings, quality burgers, and wash it down with peach and mango daiquiris. Be prepared for a wait in the evenings. *Costera Miguel Alemán, tel. 748/4–25–49. No reservations. AE, MC, V. Closed Mon. and Labor Day (May 1).*

8 Lodging

Introduction

Accommodations in Acapulco run the gamut from sprawling, big-name complexes with nonstop amenities to small, family-run inns where hot water is a luxury. Wherever you stay, prices are reasonable compared with those in the United States, and service is generally good, as Acapulcans have been catering to tourists for almost 40 years. Mexican hotels are rated by the Mexican Government on the star system, from 1- to 5-star. (Fodor's recommended accommodations are noted with one star, which is *not* based on the government's star system.) Properties with three or more stars, for example, must fulfill certain requirements, such as a TV in every room and a central location. The criteria are a little confusing, and sometimes irrelevant. A better gauge is price. Accommodations above $80 (double) are air-conditioned and include a mini-bar, TV, and a view of the bay. There is usually a range of in-house restaurants and bars as well as a pool. Exceptions exist, such as Las Brisas, which, in the name of peace and quiet, has banned TVs from all rooms. So if such extras are important to you, be sure to ask ahead. If you can't afford air-conditioning, don't panic. Even the cheapest hotels have cooling ceiling fans. Other points to keep in mind when making reservations:

● Ask for a room on one of the upper floors to avoid noise from the pool and bar areas; and on the bayside, for the view and to avoid street noise.
● Request a bath if necessary; many hotels have just showers in the majority of rooms.
● Low-season rates can mean a saving of 20–40%.
● December 24–January 4 is the height of high season, closely followed by Semana Santa (the week before Easter). Book early to avoid disappointment.

Toll-free numbers are listed for hotels that use them. If you get stuck without a room, the Department of Tourism at Costera Miguel Alemán 187 (tel. 5–13–04) can make inquiries. Unless stated, all hotels are open 365 days a year. Prices are for January 1988 and likely to change without notice.

Because Acapulco is a relatively new resort, it lacks the converted monasteries and old mansions found in Mexico City. But the "Costera" is chockablock with new luxury high rises and local franchises of major U.S. hotel chains such as Hyatt and Sheraton. Since these hotels tend to be characterless, your choice will depend on location (see below) and what facilities are available. Villa Vera, Acapulco Plaza, Las Brisas, and both Hyatts have tennis courts as well as swimming pools. The Princess and Pierre Marqués share two 18-hole golf courses, and Elcano and Malibu are across from the Club de Tennis and Golf. All major hotels can make water-sports arrangements.

In Acapulco geography is price, so where you stay determines what you pay. The most exclusive area is the East Bay, home to some of the most expensive hotels in Mexico. Travelers come here for a relaxing, self-contained holiday; the East Bay hotels are so lush and well-equipped that most guests don't budge from the minute they arrive. The minuses: Revolcadero Beach is too rough for swimming (though great for surfing and horseback riding), and the East Bay is a 15-minute (expensive) taxi ride into the heart of Acapulco. There is also very little to do in the East Bay except shop at La Vista, dine at two of Acapulco's better restaurants (Madeiras and Miramar), and dance at the glamorous Fantasy disco.

Highly recommended hotels in each price category are indicated by a star ★.

Category	Cost*
Very Expensive	$250 and up
Expensive	$95–$250
Moderate	$55–$95
Inexpensive	Under $55

All prices are for a standard double room, excluding 15% sales (called IVA) tax.

East Bay

Very Expensive **Las Brisas.** This Westin hotel, claims the dubious distinction of
★ "most expensive hotel in Mexico," but at least you get what you pay for. Privacy is a major advantage (especially rooms with a private pool) in this spread-out yet self-contained (only guests are allowed to use the facilities) luxury complex. There are 2.2 employees assigned to each room. Transportation is by white and pink jeep. You can rent one for $49 a day, including gas and insurance, or, if you don't mind a wait, the staff will do the driving. And transport is necessary—it is a good 15-minute walk to the beach restaurant, and all the facilities are far from the rooms. Everything at Las Brisas is splashed with pink, from the bedspreads and staff uniforms to the stripes in the middle of the road. Attention to detail is Las Brisas's claim to fame: Employees are collected from their homes at 4 AM so that the guest's breakfast can be put in each room's "magic box" in the early hours. Rooms are stocked with cigarettes, liquor, and snacks. Flowers are flown in daily from Mexico City to be scattered on the private pools and beds; a complimentary bowl of fresh fruit arrives each afternoon. Hotel registration takes place in a comfortable lounge to avoid lines, and Las Brisas pays the bank so that guests receive only crisp new bills. There is a small "disco" (actually a video bar), and a nouvelle Mexican restaurant (the food quality is inconsistent) overlooks the tennis courts. Lunch is taken at the often-deserted La Concha, an exclusive beach club that has two saltwater pools. There is also an art gallery, a branch of Aries leather shops, and a few other stores. Friday night is Mexican Fiesta with a rooftop buffet, razorless cockfights, and fireworks. A little Mexican village is set up, and locals selling crafts are bused in so that guests will have a chance to bargain. This, more than anything, reveals how isolated Las Brisas is, since bargaining in Mexico starts practically the moment you step off the plane. Tipping is not allowed, but $17 a day is added to the bill. *Box 281, Carretera Escénica 5255, tel. 748/4–16–50 or 800/228–3000. 300 rooms, 200 with bath. AE, DC, MC, V.*

★ **Pierre Marqués.** This hotel is doubly blessed: it is closer to the beach than any of the other East Bay hotels, and guests have access to all the Princess's facilities without the crowds. In addition, it has three pools and eight tennis courts illuminated for

Lodging

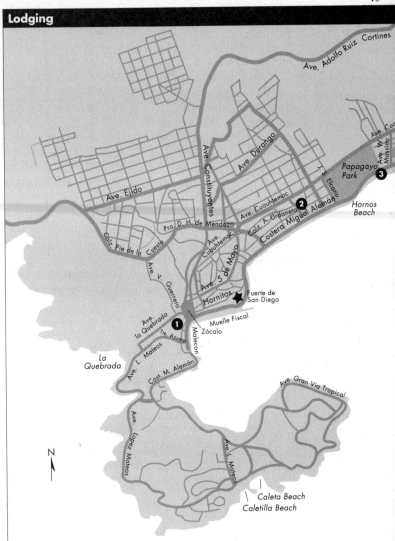

Acapulco Plaza, **7**
Acapulco Princess, **21**
Autotel Ritz, **5**
Calinda, **12**
Copacabana, **17**
Elcano, **15**

Exelaris Hyatt
Continental Acapulco, **9**
Exelaris Hyatt
Regency Acapulco, **18**
Fiesta Americana
Condesa del Mar, **11**
Gran Motel
Acapulco, **8**

Hotel Misíon, **1**
Hotel Tortuga, **10**
Las Brisas, **19**
Malibu, **14**
Maralisa, **6**
Palapa, **16**

Paraíso Radisson, **3**
Pierre Marqués, **22**
Playa Hermosa, **2**
Playa Secreto
Sheraton Acapulco, **20**
Ritz, **4**
Villa Vera, **13**

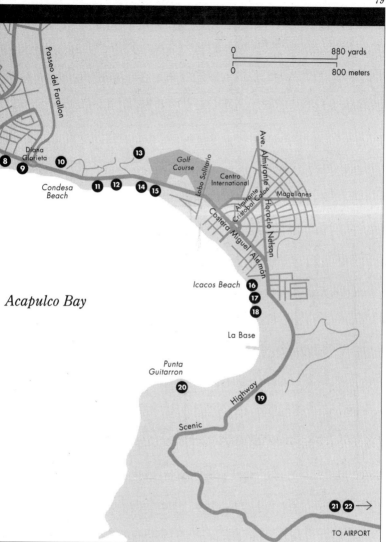

0   880 yards

0   800 meters

Passeo del Farallon

Diana Glorieta

8 9

Condesa Beach

10

13

Golf Course

Lobo Solitario

Centro International

Ave. Almirante

Almirante Cristobal Colon

Horacio Nelson

Magallanes

11 12 14 15

Costera Miguel Aleman

Acapulco Bay

Icacos Beach 16
17
18

La Base

Punta Guitarron

20

Scenic

Highway 19

21 22 →

TO AIRPORT

nighttime play. Rooms are furnished identically to those at the Princess, but duplex villas and bungalows with private patios are available. Many people stay here to relax, then hit the Princess's restaurants and discos at night—the shuttle bus runs about every ten minutes. Accommodations include breakfast and dinner. *Box 474, Playa Revolcadero, tel. 748/4–20–00 or 800/223–1818. 344 rooms with bath. AE, DC, MC, V.*

Princess. This is the first hotel you come to from the airport. A pyramid-shaped building built in 1973, the Princess has the largest capacity of any hotel in Acapulco. The hotel's fact sheet makes fascinating reading: 50 chocolate cakes are consumed daily and 2,500 staff meals are served. The Princess is one of those mega-hotels always holding at least three conventions with an ever-present horde in the lobby checking in and greeting their fellow dentists or club members. But more rooms equals more facilities. The Princess has nine restaurants, five bars, a nightclub, the Cocoloco disco, eight tennis courts, a golf course and great shopping in a cool arcade. The pool near the reception desk is sensational—fantastic tropical ponds with little waterfalls and a slatted bridge leading into a swimming/sunning area. It forms a jungle backdrop to the lobby, which is always fresh and cool from the ocean breezes. Rooms are light and airy with cane furniture and crisp yellow and green rugs and curtains. Guests can also use the facilities of its smaller sister, the Pierre Marqués; a free shuttle bus provides transport. *Box 1351 Playa Revolcadero, tel. 748/4–31–00 or 800/223–1818. 1,020 rooms, with bath. AE, DC, MC, V.*

Expensive **Playa Secreto.** The Sheraton group is finishing the construction of this new hotel in the East Bay. Very isolated with a small beach, this complex of 17 buildings (when complete) will have its own tram system for internal transport, two pools, a disco, and two tennis courts. The smallish rooms are decorated with plants and wooden furniture, some with a view of the bay. The Playa Secreto is now accepting guests, but since construction is not due to be completed until mid-1989, our advice is to steer clear. Incessant construction noise, long waits for transport, and a shortage of some catering items suggest that the opening of this Sheraton was premature. *Costera Guitarrón 110, tel. 748/4–37–37 or 800/325–3535. 315 rooms with bath. AE, DC, MC, V.*

The Strip

"Costera" is what locals call the Costera Miguel Alemán, the wide shoreline highway that leads from the bottom of the Scenic Highway, around the bay, then past old Acapulco. The Paraíso Radisson Acapulco Hotel anchors the end of The Strip. This area is where you'll find discos, American-style restaurants, airline offices, and the majority of the large hotels. It is also home base for Americans—lounging on the beaches, shopping the boutiques, and generally getting into the vacation spirit. Acapulco's best beaches are here, too. The waves are gentle and watersports are available. Hotels on the Costera take full advantage of their location. All have freshwater pools and sun decks, and most have restaurants/bars overlooking the beach, if not on the sand itself. Hotels across the street are almost always cheaper than those on the beach. And because there are no private beaches in Acapulco, all you have to do to reach the water is cross the road.

Very Expensive **Villa Vera.** A five-minute drive north of the Costera leads to one
★ of Acapulco's most exclusive hotels. Guests are primarily afflu-
ent American business travelers, actors, and politicians. This
luxury estate, officially the Villa Vera Hotel and Racquet Club,
is unequaled in the variety of its accommodations. Many re-
modeled rooms have their own pools and villas, which were
once private houses. Casa Laurel, the most exclusive, is $475 a
day. Standard rooms, in fashionable pastels and white, are not
especially large. No matter. No one spends much time in his
room. The main pool with its swim-up bar is the hotel's hub.
During the day, guests lounge, lunch, snack and swim here (a
diet menu is available for calorie-conscious guests). By night,
they dine at the terraced restaurant with its stunning view of
the bay. Though Villa Vera's guests rarely leave the premises,
taxis and tours are available. Three championship tennis
courts host the annual Miguel Alemán and Teddy Stauffer
cups. For those guests who don't have their own car, transportation is by hotel jeep. Book well in advance; guests have been
known to make reservations for the following year as they
leave. Children under 18 not allowed. *Box 560, Lomas del Mar
35, tel. 748/4-03-33 or 800/233-4895. 80 rooms with bath. AE,
DC, MC, V.*

Expensive **Acapulco Plaza.** This Holiday Inn resort is the newest and larg-
★ est hotel on the Costera. Like the Princess, the Plaza has more
facilities than many Mexican towns: 11 bars and restaurants,
four tennis courts, Jacuzzis, steam baths, and two pools. The
Galería Plaza in front of the hotel is one of the largest shopping
malls in town, rivaling that of the Princess in quality and selection. Maximilian's (*see* Dining) serves quality Continental fare.
The lobby bar is most extraordinary—a wooden hut, suspended by a cable from the roof, reached by a gangplank from
the second floor of the lobby. About 12 people can fit inside the
bar, which overlooks a garden full of flamingos and other exotic
birds. Guest rooms tell the same old story: pastels and blonde
wood replacing passé dark greens and browns. *Costera Miguel
Alemán 123, tel. 748/5-80-50 or 800/HOLIDAY. 1,008 rooms
with bath. Booked solid Dec. 20–Jan. 3, AE, DC, MC, V.*

Exelaris Hyatt Regency Acapulco. Another mega-hotel that you
never have to leave, this property is popular with business
travelers and conventioneers. (Ex-President López Portillo
used to stay in—what else—the Presidential Suite.) The
rooms are white with heavy, dark wooden furniture—a detail
that is here to stay despite the seemingly constant renovations.
Five tennis courts, five restaurants (including a beachside seafood place and a Mexican dining room), three bars, and a lavish
shopping area provide the action. The Hyatt is a little out of the
way, a plus for those who seek quiet. Rooms on the west side of
the hotel are preferable for those who want to avoid the noise of
the maneuvers at the neighboring naval base. *Costera Miguel
Alemán 1, tel. 748/4-28-08. 694 rooms with bath. AE, DC,
MC, V.*

Exelaris Hyatt Continental Acapulco. No one spends time in the
air-conditioned lobby here simply because the pool area is so
inviting. It has some of the lushest tropical foliage surrounding
the town's largest pool. A little wooden bridge leads to Fantasy
Island, and the beach is just steps away from the sun deck. A
cafeteria overlooks the whole scene, as do bayside accommodations. All rooms in this 14-story property are furnished in
"generic Acapulco"—cane headboards and adequate writing

desks. The Regency Club (10th floor) is a private level of suites, almost like a little hotel of its own. Complimentary breakfast and cocktails are served, and no children are allowed. *Box 214, Miguel Costera Alemán, tel. 748/4–09–09; 800/228–9000 (individuals); 800/492–8639 (groups). 432 rooms with bath. AE, DC, MC, V.*

Fiesta Americana Condesa del Mar. Right in the thick of the main shopping/restaurant district, the Condesa, as everyone calls it, is ever popular with tour operators. Thankfully, it has new management, which is upgrading the old dark furniture with wall-to-wall pastel plushness. Until renovation is complete, however, insist on an upper floor; air-conditioning and plumbing difficulties persist on lower levels. We have heard complaints about general upkeep of the rooms, also, but it is too early to tell if management will solve this problem. *Box 933, Costera Miguel Alemán 1220, tel. 748/4–26–03 or 800/ 228–3278. 500 rooms with bath. AE, DC, MC, V.*

Moderate   **Calinda.** Part of the Quality Inn chain, this hotel is big, popular, and well-established with a largely American following. Rooms are cheerful and light: Mexican-style mirrors, thick carpets, and flowery bedspreads and curtains are the only additions to the ubiquitous soft shades, this year's model in Acapulco. In case it isn't hot enough, the Calinda is one of the few hotels in Acapulco that has a sauna. At happy hour everyone gathers in the small lobby to enjoy the live music. The Mexican Fiesta (daily in high season; Mon., Wed., and Fri. the rest of the year) on the terrace overlooking the beach draws people from all over Acapulco who drink, partake of the buffet, and hear mariachis. *Costera Miguel Alemán 1260, tel. 748/4–04–10, 800/228–5151. 356 rooms with bath. AE, DC, MC, V.*

Copacabana. A good buy if you yearn for a modern hotel in the center of things. The staff is efficient and helpful; the ambience relaxed and festive. The lobby and pool (with a swim-up bar) are always crowded with people enjoying themselves. The psychedelic, pseudo-Mexican, lemon-and-lime hues pervade the halls and bedrooms. *Costera Miguel Alemán 130, tel. 748/4–77–30. 422 rooms, showers only. AE, DC, MC, V.*

Elcano. This hotel is set in a very peaceful recess behind the Costera, so traffic noise is not a problem. It is also right across the street from the Club de Tennis and Golf. The rooms are fairly basic; simple wooden furniture and a blue-and-orange color scheme give it an early '60s look even though it was renovated in 1987. There isn't much action here during the day; people stay on the beach rather than in the bar or lobby. Things perk up in the hotel's nightclub after dark. *Box 430, Costera Miguel Alemán, tel. 748/4–19–50. 140 rooms with bath. AE, DC, MC, V.*

Malibu. This place consists of a five- and a six-story building of time-shared apartments that are rented out when vacant. It is very popular with families who appreciate the children's pool and shaded garden. The rooms are small and, although recently renovated, not especially glamorous. Wooden shutters help the air-conditioning keep the rooms cool. No TV, but watersports and other activities can be arranged. All meals are served. *Costera Miguel Alemán 20, tel. 748/4–10–70. 80 rooms, showers only. AE, DC, MC, V.*

★ **Maralisa.** The Villa Vera's sister hotel sits on the beach side of the Costera. The sun deck surrounding two small pools—palm trees and ceramic tiles—is unusual and picturesque. The rooms have not recovered from the avocado green rage, and the body contour chairs (circa 1975) seem to have been bought in bulk from a late-night talk show host. This is a small friendly place; all rooms have TVs, and the price is right, especially since guests have access to all of Villa Vera's facilities. *Box 721, Enrique el Esclavo, tel. 748/5–66–77 or 800/233–4895. 90 rooms with bath. AE, DC, MC, V.*

Palapa. All the rooms at this hotel are suites, but the bedrooms are tiny. Round tables and a bar (you supply the booze) add to the homey feeling, and all rooms face the ocean. The beachside pool has a swim-up bar and the new health club has a weight room, sauna, massage, classes, and a juice bar. The clientele includes Mexicans, Canadians, and Americans, all here for long stays. *Fragata Yucatán 210, tel. 748/4–53–63. 341 rooms with bath. AE, DC, MC, V.*

Paraíso Radisson. The last of the big Strip hotels is a favorite of tour groups, so the lobby is forever busy. Heavy Spanish-style wooden furniture prevails in the rooms; the decorator must have loved brown and green. Guests lounge by the pool or at the beachside restaurant by day. The rooftop Fragatta restaurant provides a sensational view of the bay at night. Its intense nautical decor should not be missed by lovers of kitsch. Book early —the hotel is often full in high season with tour groups. *Costera Miguel Alemán 163, tel. 748/5–55–96 or 800/228–9822. 421 rooms with bath. AE, DC, MC, V.*

★ **Ritz.** From its brightly painted exterior it's clear that the Ritz is serious about vacations. The lobby also is seriously colorful. Parties are a hotel specialty; outdoor fiestas are held weekly, and Friday is Italian night in the lobby restaurant. Cheers is the only video bar in town. The pink and rattan rooms add to the 1950s beach-party flavor. *Box 259, Costera Miguel Alemán and Magallanes, tel. 748/5–75–44 or 800/ 527–5919. 252 rooms, half with bath. AE, DC, MC, V.*

Hotel Tortuga. A helpful staff and prime location make the "Turtle Hotel" an appealing choice. It is also one of the few non-beach hotels to have a garden (handkerchief-size) and a pool where most of the guests hang out. At night, the activity shifts to the lobby bar, with the crowd often spilling out onto the street. The downside of this merriment is the noise factor: The lower rooms open onto balconies above the lobby, while the rooms facing east enjoy regular broadcasts from the neighboring building's generator. Avoid the lower rooms on the west side of the building, which have a charming view of a large pile of rubble and a brick wall. The best bet is a room facing west on an upper floor. All rooms have blue-green pile rugs, small tables, and a working kitchen sink and refrigerator. Breakfast is served in the lobby café; lunch and dinner can be taken in the more formal restaurant. *Costera Miguel Alemán 132, tel. 748/4–88–89. 250 rooms with bath. AE, DC, MC, V.*

Inexpensive **Autotel Ritz.** The neglected relative of the Ritz is a good buy for its location. Thus it attracts bargain-hunters and senior citizens. The uncarpeted rooms are simply decorated, but the furniture is chipped and smudged with paint. Facilities include a decent-size pool with a bar; a restaurant; and room service until 9 PM. Rooms not on the Costera are quite quiet. The Autotel Ritz is recommended for those who want a fairly central location without paying top dollar. A useful note for nonguests: The long-distance surcharge is half what it is at many other hotels. *Avenue Wilfrido Massieu, Box 257, tel. 748/5-80-23. 103 rooms with bath. AE, DC, MC, V.*

Gran Motel Acapulco. This is a find for its reasonable price and central location. Bare walls and floors, and blondewood furniture give the newly decorated rooms a monastic appeal. The small pool has a bar but there is no restaurant. Ask to stay in the old section, where the rooms are larger, quieter, and have a beach view. *Costera Miguel Alemán, tel. 748/5-59-92. 87 rooms, 20 with bath. AE, DC, MC, V.*

Old Acapulco

Moving off The Strip and west along the Costera leads you to downtown Acapulco, where the fishing and tour boats depart, and the locals go about their business. The central post office, Woolworth's, and the Mercado Municipal are here, along with countless restaurants where a complete meal can cost as little as $5. The beaches here are popular with Mexican vacationers, and the dozens of little hotels attract Canadian and European bargain-hunters.

Inexpensive
★ **Hotel Misíon.** Two minutes from the Zócalo, this attractive, budget hotel is the only colonial hotel in Acapulco. The English-speaking family that runs the Misíon lives in a traditional house built in the 19th century. A new structure housing the guest rooms was added 30 years ago. It surrounds a greenery-rich courtyard with an outdoor dining area. The rooms are small and by no means fancy, with bare cement floors and painted brick walls. But every room has a shower, and sometimes there is even hot water. The Mission appears in several European guidebooks, so expect a Continental clientele. The best rooms are on the second and third floors; the top floor room is large but hot in the daytime. *Calle Felipe Valle 12, tel. 748/2-36-43. 27 rooms, showers only. AE, DC, MC, V.*

★ **Playa Hermosa.** Right behind the El Cid Hotel and steps away from Playa Hornos and the Normandie restaurant is this tiny hotel. Owner Edward Mackissack's guests return every year, so in high season rooms are hard to come by. Staying here is a good way to make friends. The mostly above-40 guests meet on the patio/dining room for drinks every night, although every spring brings a contingent of students from the University of Texas. Built in 1936, Playa Hermosa was originally Ed Mackissack's private home, and it still feels like it. Each room is unique, with a Japanese print in one, a low coffee table in the next. Even the hallways are decorated with prints and furnished with chairs. There are shelves of English books, a garden, and pool. With its Old Acapulco ambience, this is one of the more charming hotels around. All rooms have hot water, breakfast is included, and lunch can be provided if ordered the day before. *Vasco Núñez de Balboa, tel. 748/5-14-91. 20 rooms, showers only. Closed all of June. AE, DC, MC, V.*

There are dozens of ultra-cheap hotels in Old Acapulco; the enterprising, and adventurous, can find a room for as little as $1.50 a night. The main places to look are around Calle Azueta and Calle La Paz or near the Flecha Roja bus station and the Quebrada, on the hill leading up to the Mirador Hotel. Further out there are bargains to be had at the Caleta and Caletilla beaches.

Condos and Apartment Rentals

Numerous real estate agents, rental agents, and time-share companies have offices in Acapulco. Your travel agent can provide details, and the following addresses can be helpful. Prices for a three-bedroom apartment range from $150 to $250 a day and often include a pool and view of the bay. Beware of pushy salespeople. An invitation to a free breakfast is a common ploy, and when you arrive you will be set upon by avid real estate agents who will suggest that you put the first installment on your credit card. Unfortunately, management of Bella Italia (*see* Dining) has been known to let condo publicists operate from its dining room, not a welcome interruption to your dinner. Ron Lavender can arrange for villa rentals (tel. 748/5–71–51). For time-share condos, the Secretariat of Tourism recommends Napoli S.A. at Hernán Cortés 43, tel. 748/5–57–59; and Torre Playa Sol, Costera Miguel Alemán 1252, tel. 748/4–62–38 or 4–61–86. The family that owns Hotel Fiesta and Hotel Isabel also rents efficiencies. Contact Amueblados Etel, Inalambrica 42 in Old Acapulco, tel. 748/2–22–40 or 2–22–41.

9 The Arts and Nightlife

Acapulco has always been famous for its nightlife and justifiably so. For many visitors the discos and restaurants are just as important as the sun and sand. The minute the sun slips over the horizon, The Strip comes alive with people milling around window-shopping, deciding where to dine, and generally biding their time till the disco hour. Obviously you aren't going to find great culture here; theater efforts are few and far between and there is no classical music. But disco-hopping is high art in Acapulco. And for those who care to watch, there are plenty of live shows and folk dance performances. The tour companies listed in the Exploring chapter can organize evening jaunts to most of the dance and music opportunities listed below.

Entertainment

Lienza Charro, near the Princess, has shows that feature Mexican horseback riders and folkloric dances. Performances are Tuesday, Wednesday, and Saturday, at 8 PM. The cost, including dinner, is $25. Acuario Tours opposite the Plaza also organizes visits here.

The **Acapulco International Center** (also known as the convention center), has two shows nightly of mariachi bands, singers, and the "Flying Indians" from Veracruz. The show includes dinner and comes to $30. Performances begin at 7:30 and 10. "Malinche," an epic musical about the conquistadors that has received a lot of national publicity is performed nightly at 9:30. The nearby **Colonial** restaurant has a water-ski show every night at 9:30. Seafood is served while you watch. *Adults $1.50, children $1. Tel. 3–70–77 or 2–20–56.*

The famous **cliff divers** at La Quebrada perform at 1 PM (*see* Exploring) and also at 7:15, 8:15, 9:15 and 10:30 every night. Divers de México organizes sunset champagne cruises that provide a fantastic view of the spectacle from the water. For reservations, call tel. 2–13–98, or stop by the office downtown near the *Fiesta* and *Bonanza* yachts. The *Aca Tiki, Fiesta* and *Bonanza* all run nightly cruises of the bay that include dinner, drinks, and a show. All boats leave from downtown near the Zócalo. Many hotels and shops sell tickets as do the ticket-sellers on the waterfront. *Fiesta* and *Bonanza* tel. 2–20–55; *Aca tiki* tel. 4–65–70.

Don't forget the nightly entertainment at most hotels. The big resorts have live music to accompany the early-evening happy hour, and some feature big-name bands from the United States for less than you would pay at home. **Mil Luces** at the Exelaris Hyatt Regency and **Cocoloco** at the Princess are good bets for a dinner show. Many hotels sponsor theme parties, such as Italian night or beach party night. The Calinda always draws a crowd to the open-air Mexican Fiesta that features dancers, mariachis, and waiters dressed up as matadors and toros for a riotous mock bullfight. The show, dinner, and two drinks costs $20.

Dance

Nina's is a disco specializing in salsa music. On The Strip near CiCi, tel. 748/4–24–00.

Flamenco performances take place at **El Fuerte** nightclub, Costera Miguel Alemán 239, next to Las Hamacas Hotel. *Nightly, except Sun., at 10 PM, tel. 748/2-61-61.*

Film

If there is a hit movie you missed last year, chances are good that it will turn up—in English with Spanish subtitles—at one of the cinemas in town. The theaters are quite modern and comfortable; admission is about $1. Check the local papers for hours.

Cabaret

Some people enjoy the **Afrocasino,** a strip club in La Huerta, Acapulco's sleazy, depressing red-light district. All the taxi drivers know where it is. Have the waiter call you a cab when you are ready to leave. **Rebecca's** is another famous spot, where two women and one man do what's billed as a live "sex" act involving weird, and not very wonderful, activities with toilet paper.

Discos

Wherever you go you will face the question of what to drink, and because Acapulco is cocktail crazy, you have your work cut out for you. The most popular drinks are daiquiris and drinks based on tequila or rum. The local rum, when mixed with Coke, becomes the smooth and syrupy Cuba libre. Tequila and mescal are both made from the fermented juices of the maguey plant, with tequila being the smoother of the two. Tequila is the heart of a margarita or it can be mixed with 7-Up to become a popper, a local specialty. When this blend is served in a coconut shell, it is aptly named *coco loco.* Mexicans usually drink their tequila straight with salt and lemon or sometimes follow it with a beer chaser. Take note, as tequila can be very strong. Conmemorativo, the top-of-the line tequila, is a bit smoother. Gusano, a brand of mescal, comes with a worm, at the bottom of the bottle, and it makes an, ahem, unusual gift for the unlucky stay-at-homes.

Mexicans love beer, and in some working-class joints, it can cost as little as 25¢. Corona is currently fashionable in the United States, but Superior, Victoria, and Bohemia are the Buds and Millers of Mexico. Negra Modelo and Dos Equis are dark. Soft drinks are served everywhere but not so diet colas. Bottled mineral water and juices are widely available. Avoid ice if you are having stomach trouble or want to avoid having stomach trouble.

The legendary Acapulco discos are open 365 days a year from about 10:30 until they empty out, often not until 4 or 5 AM. Reservations are advisable for a big group, and late afternoon or after 9 PM are the best times to call; New Year's Eve requires advance planning.

The discos are very civilized, in that everyone gets a table and runs up a tab to be paid at the end of the night. Most clubs charge a cover (between $7 and $15), which is paid as you enter or put on your bill. The cover sometimes includes drinks, and these average $3 for local beverages and $4 for imported brands. After-dinner liqueurs run about $6, and imported champagne is the most expensive of all—$125–$150 per bottle. Many discos distribute free passes or have $10 all-you-can-drink nights, so watch for people handing them out on the street. In some places you can buy membership only for the time you are in town.

Tip just about everybody. The waiter should receive 15% of your tab or at least $4 if drinks are included in the cover charge. The headwaiter who seats you should get at least $2 or $3 before seating you, and the doorman merits $1. Tipping is a good practice if you plan to come back. Even if you don't plan to come back, remember that Mexican wages are low and that tips are salary. Leave change (about 50¢) for bathroom attendants.

Many of the discos attempt to maintain a glamorous veneer by posting outside a superior- and sullen-looking doorman who decides who may enter. Don't be intimidated; this is for appearance's sake only. You can wait outside for 10 minutes and find the place almost empty when you get in and that everyone inside is casually dressed. Some discos, such as Fantasy, don't like to have too many single men and keep them waiting until there are an equal number of single women inside. Ladies never have a problem, but if you want to meet people, the best place to sit is at the bar. Things don't really start moving till 11:30, and until people are warmed up it can take a while to be asked to dance. Those without much stamina start to leave around 2 AM, but most stick it out till 3 or 4, at least.

The best tables are those on the edge of the dance floor, and "Siberia," the worst seats, is the upper reaches away from the music. But where to sit is a subjective judgment. If you want to actually hold an audible conversation, Siberia might be more to your liking. Tables near the dance floor are often cramped and the noise level is high.

Don't worry about what to wear—no one dresses to kill in Acapulco. Fantasy is the only nightclub where people dress up, and it even seems that only women make a major effort. In general, disco garb is pretty and elegant but no one could be mistaken for a *Vogue* model. Men are accepted anywhere in slacks and a shirt. Women can wear just about anything, even shorts if they look good. The most common outfits are pastel cotton dresses or separates worn with fancy jewelry and some makeup. It is hot inside, even though the air-conditioning works, so a jacket is not necessary. Some ladies do get dolled up and the effect is always appreciated; so if you do have a slinky dress or low-cut something that you have been saving for a special occasion, wear it in Acapulco or, better yet, at Fantasy, where clubbers cultivate a sophisticated air.

Except for Fantasy, all the discos are on The Strip and, except for Le Dome, are in three different clusters. Listed from east to west they are:

Fantasy is without a doubt the most exclusive of all the discos in Acapulco. If there are any celebrities in town, they'll be here, rubbing elbows with or bumping into local fashion designers and artists—as Fantasy is quite, shall we say, snug. As we've said already, this is the only disco where people really dress up, men in well-cut pants and shirts, and the women in racy outfits and cocktail dresses. The crowd is 25–50 and mainly in couples. Singles gravitate to the two bars in the back. A line sometimes forms, so people come here earlier than to other places. By midnight the dance floor is so packed that people dance on the wide windowsills that look out over the bay. At 2 AM there is a fireworks display. Capacity is 300, so although seating is cramped, all seats have a view of the floor. "Siberia" consists of an upstairs balcony. Around the floor are long plastic tubes filled with illuminated bubbles and there is a good light show. In spite of everyone's proximity to the sound system, it is just possible to have a conversation—although not about anything complicated. A glassed-in elevator provides an interesting overview of the scene and leads upstairs to a little shop that stocks T-shirts and lingerie. *On the Scenic Highway, next to Las Brisas, tel. 748/4–63–45.*

Magic is all black inside and has a fabulous light show each night after midnight. This is a good-size place with tables on tiers looking down at the floor. This is one of the few discos where on weekdays you can find a fair number of Mexicans. Any day of the week this is a good bet to catch up on the Top 10 from Mexico City as well as the American dance hits. The atmosphere is friendly and laid-back. *Across the Costera from Baby O, tel. 748/4–88–15.*

Baby O and Le Dome (*see* below) are the hot spots of the moment. Even mid-week, Baby O is packed. The dance floor is a New York City subway at rush hour, the bar is Grand Central Terminal. Coming here is not a comfortable experience, nor is it quiet or peaceful; it is total chaos. Baby O bucks the trend of most discos in Acapulco. Instead of the usual mirrors and glitz, Baby O resembles a cave in a tropical jungle, with simple plants and walls made of a strange stonelike substance. The crowd is 18–30 and mostly tourists, although many Mexicans come here, too. In fact, this is one of Acapulco's legendary pick-up spots, so feel free to ask someone to dance. When the pandemonium gets to you, retreat to the little hamburger restaurant. Watch your step at all times, however, to avoid falling on the tables and waiters. The architect clearly thought he was designing for acrobats. *Costera Miguel Alemán 22, tel. 748/4–74–74.*

Bocaccio's is an institution on The Strip. The enormous blue-and-white illuminated sign is impossible to miss. Inside, it is all mirrors and spangles, streamers and confetti. Customers have been coming here for years, and the champagne-loving owner, Aaron, often sits at a booth by the dance floor greeting regulars. The crowd is a little older and even near the dance floor it is possible to chat. But don't get the idea that the place is sedate. Bocaccio's has a loyal following and when people come, they don't leave until late. Before you head home, stop at the shop—one of the larger disco shops around—and check out the logo sweatshirts. *Costera Miguel Alemán 5040, tel. 748/4–19–00, or 4–19–01.*

Le Dome, an Acapulco standby, is more popular than ever. Even before the music starts at 11:30, there is already a small crowd at the door, and in spite of the capacity of 800, this club is always full. Le Dome doesn't look very different from other clubs on The Strip—it has the usual black wall and mirror mix, although it does have a larger video screen than most. Le Dome is the only club in Acapulco, if not in the world, where you can play *basketball*, yes, basketball, every Wed. Winners get a bottle of tequila. *Next door to Fiorucci, tel. 748/4–11–90.*

Discobeach is Acapulco's only alfresco disco and also its most informal. The under-30 crowd sometimes even turns up in shorts. The waiters are all young and friendly, and every night they dress to a different theme. One night they're all in togas carrying bunches of grapes, the next they're in pajamas. Other nights feature a Hawaiian luau or a mock bullfight. Every Wed., ladies' night, all the women receive flowers. Happy hour runs early at Discobeach, from 7:30-10:30. The *coco loco* is the house special. *On The Strip, one minute east of Eve's, tel. 748/4–70–64.*

Eve's caters to the energetic. Chava, the manager, loves to keep his guests busy. Weekends it's nonstop dancing on the dance floor, in the aisles, and every level surface within earshot of the DJ. But weeknights he throws imaginative theme parties (a photo album recalls the better moments). On wine nights, waiters pour the liquid grape down guests' throats from a traditional Spanish long-necked *porrón*. Argentine dancers, male and female (partial) striptease artists, and go-go dancers entertain on other nights. Chava dotes on crazy games, and the winners get bottles of booze. A video camera records the action so those at the bar and those waiting to get in can see what they are missing on the dance floor. *Costera Miguel Alemán 115, tel. 748/4–47–78.*

Jackie O has pretensions to all the glamour of the great lady herself, though one can only imagine what she thinks of this disco or the bathrooms, preciously dubbed "Jackie O" and "Aristotle." A tuxedoed doorman guards the red carpeted stairs that lead to the entrance. Once inside you can dance, shop for accessories and T-shirts, or watch the two large video screens. At 2 AM, balloons, streamers, and free poppers announce the nightly limbo party. Comfortable is the operative word here; big booths and wrap-around sofas all have a view of the dance floor. Lasers and lights penetrate the seating area without irritating, and there are numerous relatively quiet spaces. *Opposite the Ritz Hotel, tel. 748/4–87–33.*

Midnight is very sophisticated. The seats are comfortable armchairs and sofas with a good view for people-watching. The managers wear suits, and the disco is an art gallery—the walls are covered with tasteful renditions of the beach and other typical Mexican scenes. In addition to the usual videos and disco music, mariachi bands make an appearance after midnight. This club is less crowded than most. There is always room to dance. *Just behind Jackie O, tel. 748/4–82–95.*

Cats is owned by the people responsible for Jackie O, and is one of the prettier places in town. It's all basic black, with half-moon lights dangling from "trees," overstuffed sofas by the bathrooms, and painted mannequins at the entrance. Service is supremely efficient. Waiters take drinks to the dance floor and appear with refills as soon as you are ready. Late into the night the headwaiter often dances in the aisles with the customers. Best of all, several nights a week the $10 cover includes all you can drink. Poppers are served with a flourish—customers don hard hats, and the drink is mixed by hitting the protected head.

Once Cats gets going the atmosphere is very congenial, and no one leaves without having talked to most of the people sitting nearby. *Juan de la Cosa 32, tel. 748/4-72-35.*

Cheers is Acapulco's only video bar, so those who don't dance head here. The bar is sleek and spare. Entertainment comes from the little TVs and large screens televising everything from music videos to Indonesian dancers. Cheers has a satellite hookup and gets all the sports coverage from the United States and Canada. There are several long bars where people meet. Service is excellent. Big bowls of nuts are provided, and all you have to do is think about smoking to get the waiters to light a match. For a colorful drink, ask for manager Jesús Guerrero's Ticket to Fly, a suave, but not too lethal combination of tequila, gin, rum, vodka, beer, and "cream of love" (lavender water). *Ritz Hotel, Costera Miguel Alemán and Magallanes, tel. 748/5-73-36, ext. 10100.*

10 Excursions

Roqueta Island

A respite from the crowds on the main beaches, Roqueta Island is visited mainly by Mexicans. Ask your taxi driver to take you to the *embarcadero* (wharf) near Caleta and Caletilla beaches. From there you can see the island—a mere 10 minutes away by motorboat. Tickets are available from specially designated offices and from boys with their own ticket books. Contrary to what is printed on the ticket, the price should be about $1.25 round-trip. When you buy your ticket ask which boat it is for, because each company's boat is marked with a different color. Retain the stub; it is for your return trip. For about $2.50 you can buy a ticket for the glass-bottomed boat that takes 45 minutes and detours for a look at the marine life as well as the sunken statue of the Virgin of Guadalupe. The last boat from Roqueta back to the mainland leaves at 5 PM.

Once on Roqueta there are several simple restaurants frequented by Mexicans. The energetic may want to make the half-hour climb up to the *faro* (lighthouse). It is an overgrown route and fairly strenuous, but the view at the top makes up for it—from there you have a bird's-eye view of the entire bay. Just take the walkway to the right of the landing and proceed upward.

If you bear right and walk for about five minutes along a rather narrow, broken-down walkway (damaged in a fire and not for the fainthearted), you will eventually reach Palao's, a palapa-roof restaurant that serves lobster and fish caught in the bay in front of the restaurant. A two-course lunch will cost about $12. Palao's is decorated with all sorts of tribal paintings and motifs, and the effect is that of inside a tropical hut. It is popular with tour operators, so if you arrive when there is a group here, you may catch the performance of Indian dances. This tour is not recommended, though, as the buffet served to groups is of very poor quality and includes a locally caught shellfish that most fishermen usually toss back. Come alone and choose what you eat. Palao's has its own little cove—alas, sometimes very polluted—and offers snorkeling and scuba diving equipment for rent. Local fishermen, displaying homemade shell sculptures, stand in the water with their boats and will take you for a paddle around the bay. Children love Palao's because there is a cage of monkeys and a friendly little horse they can pet. If you want to come only to Palao and not to the rest of Roqueta, don't pay for a boat ticket. Palao has its own motorboat, *Conejo (The Rabbit)*, which leaves from Caleta and Caletilla. *Open daily for lunch. AE, DC, MC, V. Groups require reservations, tel. 748/2–11–14.*

Pie de la Cuesta

About a 15-minute drive from Old Acapulco, this beach has the advantage of being right next to Coyuca Lagoon. The water here is too rough for swimming, but Pie de la Cuesta is famous for its sensational sunsets. The road turns off the Costera at the Artisans' Market and then goes west, with a view of the ocean. In town, just follow the signs to Pie de la Cuesta (they are easy to miss) and take the Pie de la Cuesta turnoff when you arrive.

Or hire a taxi and try not to pay more than $15 plus tip. The beach is pretty and fairly empty of people, but the lagoon is a complete surprise: a luscious blue surrounded by dense vegetation and birds. There are several restaurants on both the lagoon and the beach side, so it is easy to spend the day; this is also the place for freshwater fishing. If you want to spend the night also, there are two hotels, (*see* below). Tres Marías, on the lagoon, is a little club where you can rent a boat for waterskiing or for trips on the lagoon. The price is about $25 an hour. You can also rent a two-man hang glider at the rate of $30 for 15 minutes. If Tres Marías is crowded, order lunch when you arrive for whatever time you prefer.

Next door to Tres Marías is Cadena's Club Náutico. Besides ski and excursion boats for $20 an hour, you may also choose from backgammon and ping-pong. Some people cross back over to the beach during the day for sunbathing and beachside drinks. Or rent a hammock to lounge in for $1.50, or as little as 30¢ at Hotel Casablanca. Whenever you come, though, be sure and stay for the sunset. The sight is dramatic and many applaud when it is over.

There are two little hotels at Pie de la Cuesta. Casablanca is a very simple family-run operation with rooms for $15 a day and a restaurant that serves all meals. *Book in advance by writing: Bungalows y Restaurante Casablanca, Playa Pie de la Cuesta 3270, Acapulco, Guerrero, Mexico.*

The more upscale Ukae Kim is a collection of small buildings surrounded by a shaded garden. Guests spend time at the pool and beachside bar, both of which are open to visitors for $1.50. Here also are nine rooms, a restaurant, and sometimes barbecues on the beach.

Off the Beaten Track

Popular though Pie de la Cuesta is, tourists rarely venture beyond to the western part of Coyuca and the isolated, flower-filled lagoon. Once you get to Pie de la Cuesta, follow the road down; turn right before you get to the end of the road and the army base. This is a rough, bumpy, dirt road. Drive for half an hour until you can't go any farther and you will come upon a remarkable place: a whole village of fishermen who continue their lives practically untouched by the tourist explosion in Acapulco. The community has its own little church and cluster of houses, and the people are friendly and will take you for boat rides on the lagoon. The price varies, however, so ask at your hotel or at one of the restaurants, and be prepared to bargain. There are several small seafood restaurants, and most managers will be happy to lend you a hammock if you want to spend the night.

Nothing remains untouched in Acapulco for long, and it is only a matter of time before the western tip of the lagoon will be developed. On the dirt road leading to the fishing village is a tiny hotel, Malebba's Beach Club, (tel. 748/5–84–72) at Playa Mogote. It is the first of what will probably be many small hotels in the near future. Tour operators book it already, but it is still an ideal place to hole up for a few days of isolation. There is a small pool, a buffet lunch served daily at 2, and a tennis

court. Scheduled for completion by early 1989 are 10 hotel
rooms, a water slide for children, and tables for billiards and
ping-pong. Even if you don't stay the night, partake of the
lunchtime seafood menu. It is about half what it would cost in
town.

Spanish Vocabulary and Menu

Words and Phrases

	English	*Spanish*	*Pronunciation*
Basics	Yes/no	Sí/no	see/no
	Please	Por favor	pore fah-**vore**
	May I?	Me permite?	may pair-**meh**-tay
	Thank you (very much)	(Muchas) gracias	(**moo**-chas) **grah**-see-as
	You're welcome	De nada	day **nah**-dah
	Excuse me	Con permiso	cone pair-**me**-so
	Pardon me/what did you say?	Perdón?/Mande?	pair-**doan**/ **mahn**-deh
	Could you tell me?	Podría decirme?	po-**dree**-ah deh-**seer**-meh
	I'm sorry	Lo siento	lo see-**en**-toe
	Good morning!	Buenos días!	**bway**-noss **dee**-ahs
	Good afternoon!	Buenas tardes!	**bway**-nahs **tar**-dess
	Good evening!	Buenas noches!	**bway**-nuss **no**-chess
	Goodbye!	Adiós!	ah-dee-**ohss**
	Mr./Mrs	Señor/Señora	sen-**yore**/ sen-**yore**-ah
	Miss	Señorita	sen-yo-**ree**-tuh
	Pleased to meet you	Mucho gusto	**moo**-cho **goose**-toe
	How are you?	Cómo está usted?	ko-mo es-**tah**, oo-**sted**
	Very well, thank you.	Muy bien, gracias.	**moo**-ee bee-**en grah**-see-us
	And you?	Y usted?	ee oos-**ted?**
	Hello (on the telephone)	Bueno	**buen**-oh
Numbers	one	uno	**oo**-no
	two	dos	dos
	three	tres	trace
	four	cuatro	**kwah**-tro
	five	cinco	**sink**-oh
	six	seis	sace
	seven	siete	see-**et**-eh
	eight	ocho	**O**-cho
	nine	nueve	new-**ev**-ay
	ten	diez	dee-**es**
Days of the week	Sunday	domingo	doe-**meen**-goh
	Monday	lunes	**loo**-ness
	Tuesday	martes	**mahr**-tess
	Wednesday	miércoles	me-air-koh-less
	Thursday	jueves	who-**ev**-ess
	Friday	viernes	vee-**air**-ness
	Saturday	sábado	**sah**-bah-doe
Months of the year	January	enero	eh-**neh**-ro
	February	febrero	feh-**brair**-oh

	English	Spanish	Pronunciation
	March	marzo	**mahr**-so
	April	abril	ah-**breel**
	May	mayo	**my**-oh
	June	junio	**hoon**-nee-oh
	July	julio	**who**-lee-yoh
	August	agosto	ah-**ghost**-toe
	September	septiembre	sep-**teem**–breh
	October	octubre	oak-**too**-breh
	November	noviembre	no-**veem**-breh
	December	diciembre	dee-see-**em**-breh
Useful phrases	Do you speak English?	¿Habla usted inglés?	**ah**-blah oos-**ted** in-**glehs**?
	I don't speak Spanish	No hablo español	no **ah**-blow es-pahn-**yol**
	I don't understand (you)	No entiendo	no en-tee-**en**-doe
	I understand (you)	Entiendo	en-tee-**en**-doe
	I don't know	No sé	no **seh**
	I am American/British	Soy americano(a)/ britanico(a)	soy ah-may-ree-**kah**-no(ah)
	What's your name?	¿Cómo se llama usted?	**koh**-mo say **yah**-mah oos-**ted**?
	My name is . . .	Me llamo . . .	meh **yah**-mo
	What time is it?	¿Qué hora es?	keh **o**-rah es?
	It is one, two, three . . . o'clock.	Es la una, son las dos . . . tres	es la **oo**-nuh/sone lahs dose . . . trace
	Yes, please/No, thank you.	Sí, por favor/No, gracias	**see** pore fah-**vor**/no **grah**-see-us
	How?	¿Cómo?	**koh**-mo?
	When?	¿Cuándo?	**kwahn**-doe?
	This/Next week	Esta semana/próxima semana	**es**-tah seh-**mah**-nuh/ **proke**-see-muh say-**mah**-nuh
	This/Next month	Este mes/el próximo mes	**es**-tay mess/el **proke**-see-mo mess
	This/Next year	Este año/el año que viene	**es**-tay **on**-yo/el **on**-yo kay vee-**yen**-ay
	Yesterday/today/ tomorrow	Ayer/hoy/mañana	ah-**yair**/oy/mahn-**yah**-nah
	This morning/ afternoon	Esta mañana/ tarde	**es**-tuh mahn-**yah**-nah/ **tar**-deh
	Tonight	Esta noche	**es**-tuh **no**-cheh
	What?	¿Qué?	kay

English	Spanish	Pronunciation
What is it?	¿Qué es esto?	Kay es **es**-toe
Why?	¿Por qué?	pore **kay**
Who?	¿Quién?	kee-**yen**
Where is . . . ?	¿Dónde está . . . ?	**dohn**-day es-**tah**
the train station?	la estación del tren?	la es-tah-see-**on** del **train**
the subway station?	la estación del Metro?	la es-tah-see-**on** del **met**-ro
the bus stop?	la parada del camión?	la pah-**rah**-duh del kah-mee-**on**
the post office?	el correo?	el koh-**reh**-oh
the bank?	el banco?	el **bahn**-koh
the . . . hotel?	el hotel . . . ?	el oh-**tel**
the store?	la tienda . . . ?	la tee-**en**-duh
the cashier?	la caja?	la **kah**-huh
the . . . museum?	el museo . . . ?	el moo-**seh**-oh
the hospital?	el hospital?	el ohss-pea-**tal**
the elevator?	el ascensor?	el ah-**sen**-sore
the bathroom?	el baño?	el **bahn**-yoh
Here/there	Aquí/al lá	ah-**key**/ah-**yah**
Open/closed	Abierto/cerrado	ahb-**yer**-toe/ser-**ah**-doe
Left/right	Izquierda/derecha	is-key-**er**-duh/ dare-**eh**-chuh
Straight ahead	Derecho	der-**eh**-choh
Is it near/far?	¿Está cerca/lejos?	es-**tah** **sair**-kah/ **lay**-hohss
I'd like . . .	Quisiera . . .	kee-sce-air-uh
a room	un cuarto	oon **kwahr**-toe
the key	la llave	lah **yah**-veh
a newspaper	un periódico	oon pear-ee-**oh**-dee-koh
a stamp	un timbre de correo	oon **team**-bray day koh-**ray**-oh
to buy . . .	comprar . . .	kohm-**prahr**
cigarettes	cigarros	see-**gah**-rohss
matches	cerillas	ser-**ee**-as
a dictionary	un diccionario	oon deek-see-oh-**nah**-ree-oh
soap	jabón	hah-**bone**
a map	un mapa	oon **mah**-pah
a magazine	una revista	**oon**-ah reh-**veess**-tah
paper	papel	pah-**pel**
envelopes	sobres	**so**-brace
a postcard	una tarjeta postal	**oon**-ah tar-**het**-uh post-**ahl**

English	Spanish	Pronunciation 100
How much is it?	¿Cuánto cuesta?	**kwahn**-toe **kwes**-tuh
It's expensive/ cheap	Está caro/barato	es-**tah kah**-roh/ bah-**rah**-toe
A little/a lot	Un poquito/ demasiado . . .	oon poh-**kee**-toe/ day-mah-see-**ah**-doe
More/less enough/too much/too little	Más/menos Suficiente/ demasiado/ muy poco	mahss/**men**-ohss soo-fee-see-**en**-tay/day-mah-see-**ah**-doe/ **moo**-ee poh-koh
Telephone	Teléfono	tel-**ef**-oh-no
Telegram	Telegrama	tay-lay-**grah**-muh
I am ill/sick	Estoy enfermo(a)	es-**toy** en-**fair**-moh(ah)
Please call a doctor	Por favor llame un médico	pore fa-**vor** ya-may ah **med**-ee-koh
Help!	¡Auxilio!	owk-**see**-lee-oh
Fire!	¡Encendio!	en-**sen**-dee-oo
Caution!/Look out!	¡Cuidado!	kwee-**dah**-doh
A bottle of . . .	Una botella de . . .	**oo**-nah bo-**tay**-yah deh
A cup of . . .	Una taza de . . .	**oo**-nah **tah**-sah deh
A glass of . . .	Un vaso de . . .	oon **vah**-so day
Ashtray	Un cenicero	oon sen-ee-**say**-roh
Bill/check	La cuenta	lah **kwen**-tuh
Bread	El pan	el pahn
Breakfast	El desayuno	el day-sigh-**oon**-oh
Butter	La mantequilla	lah mahn-tay-**key**-yah
Cheers!	¡Salud!	sah-**lood**
Cocktail	Un aperitivo	oon ah-pair-ree-**tee**-voh
Dinner	La cena	lah **seh**-nah
Dish	Un plato	oon **plah**-toe
Dish of the day	El platillo de hoy	el plah-**tee**-yo day oy
Enjoy!	¡Buen provecho!	bwen pro-**veh**-cho
Fixed-price menu	La comida corrida	lah koh-**me**-duh co-**ree**-dah
Fork	El tenedor	el ten-ay-**door**
I am diabetic	Yo soy diabético(a)	soy dee-ah-**bet**-ee-koh(ah)
I am on a diet	Estoy a dieta	es-**toy** ah dee-**et**-ah

English	Spanish	Pronunciation
I am vegetarian	Soy vegetariano(a)	soy vay-hay-tah-ree-**ah**-noh(ah)
I cannot eat . . .	No puedo comer . . .	no **pwed**-oh koh-**mare**
I am ready to order	Voy a ordenar	voy ah or-den-**are**
I'd like to order	Me gustaría ordenar . . .	may goose-tah-**ree**-ah or-den-**are**
I'm hungry/thirsty	Tengo hambre/sed	**ten**-go **ahm**-breh/sed
Is the tip included?	¿Está incluida la propina?	es-**tah** in-clue-**ee**-dah lah pro-**pea**-nah
It's good It's bad	Está bueno No está bueno	es-**tah** bway-no no es-**tah** bway-no
It's hot/cold	Está caliente/frío	es-**tah** kah-lee-**en**-tay/ **free**-oh
Knife	El cuchillo	el koo-**chee**-yo
Lunch	La comida	lah koh-**me**-dah
Menu	La carta	lah **cart**-ah
Napkin	La servilleta	lah sair-vee-**yet**-uh
Pepper	La pimienta	lah pea-me-**en**-tah
Please give me	Por favor déme	pore fah-**vor** **day**-may
Salt	La sal	lah sahl
Spoon	Una cuchara	**oo**-nah koo-**chah**-ruh
Sugar	El azúcar	el lah-**sue**-car
Waiter!/Waitress!	¡Por favor Señor/Señorita	pore fah-**vor** sen-**yor**/sen-yor-ee-tah
The wine list	La lista de vinos	lah **lees**-tah deh **vee**-nos

Conversion Tables

Distance

Miles/Kilometers To change miles to kilometers, multiply miles by 1.61.
To change kilometers to miles, multiply kilometers by .621.

Km to Mi	Mi to Km
1 = .62	1 = 1.6
2 = 1.20	2 = 3.2
3 = 1.9	3 = 4.8
4 = 2.5	4 = 6.4
5 = 3.2	5 = 8.1
6 = 3.8	6 = 9.8
7 = 4.4	7 = 11.4
8 = 5.1	8 = 13.0
9 = 5.7	9 = 14.6

Feet/Meters To change feet to meters, multiply feet by .305.
To change meters to feet, multiply meters by 3.28.

Meters to Feet	Feet to Meters
1 = 3.3	1 = .31
2 = 6.6	2 = .61
3 = 9.8	3 = .92
4 = 13.1	4 = 1.2
5 = 16.4	5 = 1.5
6 = 19.7	6 = 1.8
7 = 23.0	7 = 2.1
8 = 26.2	8 = 2.5
9 = 29.5	9 = 2.8

Liquid Volume

U.S. Gallons/Liters To change U.S. gallons to liters, multiply gallons by 3.79.
To change liters to U.S. gallons, multiply liters by .264.

Liters to U.S. Gal.	U.S. Gal. to Liters
1 = .26	1 = 3.8
2 = .53	2 = 7.6
3 = 7.9	3 = 11.4
4 = 1.1	4 = 15.1
5 = 1.3	5 = 18.9
6 = 1.6	6 = 22.7
7 = 1.8	7 = 26.5

Index

Personal Itinerary

Departure *Date*

Time

Transportation

Arrival *Date*   *Time*

Departure *Date*   *Time*

Transportation

Accommodations

Arrival *Date*   *Time*

Departure *Date*   *Time*

Transportation

Accommodations

Arrival *Date*   *Time*

Departure *Date*   *Time*

Transportation

Accommodations

Personal Itinerary

Arrival *Date*   *Time*

Departure *Date*   *Time*

Transportation

Accommodations

Arrival *Date*   *Time*

Departure *Date*   *Time*

Transportation

Accommodations

Arrival *Date*   *Time*

Departure *Date*   *Time*

Transportation

Accommodations

Arrival *Date*   *Time*

Departure *Date*   *Time*

Transportation

Accommodations

Personal Itinerary

Arrival *Date*   *Time*

Departure *Date*   *Time*

Transportation

Accommodations

Arrival *Date*   *Time*

Departure *Date*   *Time*

Transportation

Accommodations

Arrival *Date*   *Time*

Departure *Date*   *Time*

Transportation

Accommodations

Arrival *Date*   *Time*

Departure *Date*   *Time*

Transportation

Accommodations

Addresses

Name	*Name*
Address	*Address*
Telephone	*Telephone*
Name	*Name*
Address	*Address*
Telephone	*Telephone*
Name	*Name*
Address	*Address*
Telephone	*Telephone*
Name	*Name*
Address	*Address*
Telephone	*Telephone*
Name	*Name*
Address	*Address*
Telephone	*Telephone*
Name	*Name*
Address	*Address*
Telephone	*Telephone*
Name	*Name*
Address	*Address*
Telephone	*Telephone*
Name	*Name*
Address	*Address*
Telephone	*Telephone*

Fodor's Travel Guides

U.S. Guides

Alaska
American Cities
The American South
Arizona
Atlantic City & the
  New Jersey Shore
Boston
California
Cape Cod
Carolinas & the
  Georgia Coast
Chesapeake
Chicago
Colorado
Dallas & Fort Worth
Disney World & the
  Orlando Area

The Far West
Florida
Greater Miami,
  Fort Lauderdale,
  Palm Beach
Hawaii
Hawaii (Great Travel
  Values)
Houston & Galveston
I-10: California to
  Florida
I-55: Chicago to New
  Orleans
I-75: Michigan to
  Florida
I-80: San Francisco to
  New York

I-95: Maine to Miami
Las Vegas
Los Angeles, Orange
  County, Palm Springs
Maui
New England
New Mexico
New Orleans
New Orleans (Pocket
  Guide)
New York City
New York City (Pocket
  Guide)
New York State
Pacific North Coast
Philadelphia
Puerto Rico (Fun in)

Rockies
San Diego
San Francisco
San Francisco (Pocket
  Guide)
Texas
United States of
  America
Virgin Islands
  (U.S. & British)
Virginia
Waikiki
Washington, DC
Williamsburg,
  Jamestown &
  Yorktown

Foreign Guides

Acapulco
Amsterdam
Australia, New Zealand
  & the South Pacific
Austria
The Bahamas
The Bahamas (Pocket
  Guide)
Barbados (Fun in)
Beijing, Guangzhou &
  Shanghai
Belgium & Luxembourg
Bermuda
Brazil
Britain (Great Travel
  Values)
Canada
Canada (Great Travel
  Values)
Canada's Maritime
  Provinces
Cancún, Cozumel,
  Mérida, The
  Yucatán
Caribbean
Caribbean (Great
  Travel Values)

Central America
Copenhagen,
  Stockholm, Oslo,
  Helsinki, Reykjavik
Eastern Europe
Egypt
Europe
Europe (Budget)
Florence & Venice
France
France (Great Travel
  Values)
Germany
Germany (Great Travel
  Values)
Great Britain
Greece
Holland
Hong Kong & Macau
Hungary
India
Ireland
Israel
Italy
Italy (Great Travel
  Values)
Jamaica (Fun in)

Japan
Japan (Great Travel
  Values)
Jordan & the Holy Land
Kenya
Korea
Lisbon
Loire Valley
London
London (Pocket Guide)
London (Great Travel
  Values)
Madrid
Mexico
Mexico (Great Travel
  Values)
Mexico City & Acapulco
Mexico's Baja & Puerto
  Vallarta, Mazatlán,
  Manzanillo, Copper
  Canyon
Montreal
Munich
New Zealand
North Africa
Paris
Paris (Pocket Guide)

People's Republic of
  China
Portugal
Province of Quebec
Rio de Janeiro
The Riviera (Fun on)
Rome
St. Martin / St. Maarten
Scandinavia
Scotland
Singapore
South America
South Pacific
Southeast Asia
Soviet Union
Spain
Spain (Great Travel
  Values)
Sweden
Switzerland
Sydney
Tokyo
Toronto
Turkey
Vienna
Yugoslavia

Special-Interest Guides

Bed & Breakfast
  Guide: North America
1936...On the
  Continent

Royalty Watching
Selected Hotels of
  Europe

Selected Resorts
  and Hotels of the U.S.
Ski Resorts of North
  America

Views to Dine by
  around the World

Join us in updating the next edition of your Fodor's guide

Title of Guide:

1 Hotel ☐ Restaurant ☐ *(check one)*

Name

Number/Street

City/State/Country

Comments

2 Hotel ☐ Restaurant ☐ *(check one)*

Name

Number/Street

City/State/Country

Comments

3 Hotel ☐ Restaurant ☐ *(check one)*

Name

Number/Street

City/State/Country

Comments

Your Name *(optional)*

Address

General Comments

Business Reply Mail

First Class   *Permit Nº 7775*   *New York, NY*

Postage will be paid by addressee

Fodor's Travel Publications

201 East 50th Street
New York, NY 10022